NEW COMMUNITIES, NEW MINISTRIES

MICHEL BAVAREL

NEW COMMUNITIES, NEW MINISTRIES

The Church Resurgent
in Asia, Africa, and Latin America

Translated from the French
by Francis Martin

ORBIS BOOKS
Maryknoll, New York 10545

The Catholic Foreign Mission Society of America (Maryknoll) recruits and trains people for overseas missionary service. Through Orbis Books Maryknoll aims to foster the international dialogue that is essential to mission. The books published, however, reflect the opinions of their authors and are not meant to represent the official position of the society.

First published as *Chrétiens du bout du monde*, copyright © 1980 by Editions Cana, 52 rue Servan, 75011 Paris, France

English translation copyright © 1983 by Orbis Books, Maryknoll, NY 10545
Manufactured in the United States of America

Library of Congress Cataloging in Publication Data

Bavarel, Michel.
  New communities, new ministries.

  Translation of: Chrétiens du bout du monde.
  1. Church and underdeveloped areas—Catholic Church.
2. Catholic Church—History—20th century. I. Title.
BX1401.A1B3813   1983   282'.09172'4   82-22318
ISBN 0-88344-337-6 (pbk.)

CONTENTS

INTRODUCTION

First of all, I should like to take you to the Harar region of Ethiopia.

We pass long columns of pilgrims making their way along a dusty road; others are trudging up and down the fields. The women are bowed under the loads they carry. There are tens of thousands of persons—the newspapers will say one hundred twenty thousand—all converging on a desolate mountain. They arrive by train, by plane, by bus, by car, by taxi—and on foot.

It is the vigil of the feast of St. Gabriel. The archangel hears prayers—better than does God the Father—and performs miracles, especially that of healing barren women. At the top of the mountain, some nine thousand feet high, there is an enormous church built at the end of the last century to commemorate a victory of the Christians over the Moslems. This, of course, in no way prevents Moslems from participating in the pilgrimage.

All around the church there is a huge campsite with tents scattered over the grassy slopes and parking areas for cars and buses. A huge black cloud hovers threateningly overhead, while the fog blends in with the smoke from thousands of fires that have been lit to make tea. Soon a thin, icy rain beats down on us. All along the roads, now long veins of mud, there are beggars wrapped in *shammas* (cotton cloaks) gray with dirt.

You go behind some wall inside yourself and risk a few furtive glances. The shock of the whole scene is just too violent: it seems as though all the misery of the world has assembled on this mountain. There are legless amputees pulling themselves along the ground, persons with elephantiasis, all sorts of sick, especially lepers—hundreds of lepers holding out their stumps as you pass. You wander among them like a sleepwalker, your throat tight, weeping but not with tears.

1

Lines form in front of a small building with three windows in it. Through one, they throw silver and gold; through the second, rich embroidered cloth; through the third, incense. They are thanking St. Gabriel. Groups of youngsters dance and sing as they go round the church. Every once in a while the strident calls of the women reverberate. Furnished with a microphone, a priest of the Ethiopian church exhorts the faithful.

Night comes. In a hollow of the valley, there is a film being projected onto an enormous screen. Under the tents, crackers and beer are for sale. Someone invites us to come closer to the fire; a man standing there warming his hands knows a few words of French. "I had no wife. I asked St. Gabriel and he gave me a wife. I asked him for children and now I have four. That is why I come here every year, out of gratitude."

Soon everyone prepares for the night. The grass is wet, and so are the blankets they lend us—naively we left in the morning with just sweaters. Later that night, when I could not stand the cold any longer, I took refuge in the crowded church. There were mothers with their babies, old men and women sound asleep, all on the bare floor. In the choir, priests dressed in brilliant robes were singing a slow chant: I would hear it again hours later.

As I made my way back to stretch out by the dead ashes of the fire, I could see the ground strewn with what looked like large gray stones: they were the bodies of the sleepers wrapped in their *shammas* as in winding sheets. A baby was crying. Then the rain began again, this time heavy and incessant.

Pierced to the bone with cold and rain, we tried to get out of it, accompanied by a rushing stream of mud. A beggar lay beside the road making a figure S on the ground. When we went by earlier that night he had been there in the same position.

•

I looked at my watch. Another day had begun; it is one o'clock in the morning. I had asked Workeye (pronounced vor-kee-yee) to wake me up at four thirty, never thinking that, if he always came on time for our meetings during the day, it was thanks to the sun. But in the middle of this dark night, he guides me through the network of paths that crisscross the tiny village of Lalibela in the heart of Christian Ethiopia.

Workeye must be about fourteen years old. He lives with his mother and sister in a shed attached to a mud hut. The walls are branches of a eucalyptus tree and the roof is a piece of tin sheeting; there is a fireplace, and that is all, or practically all, you see. They sleep on the ground. To support the family, Workeye's mother goes out early every morning to the mountain and comes back about noon loaded down with a bundle of branches that she sells for the equivalent of fifty cents.

We go alone between a double row of beggars; they groan a bit as we pass. Next, we take a log bridge over a ditch and slip through narrow alleys until we finally arrive at an open esplanade. We are now at the center of an extraordinary complex of eleven monolithic churches excavated rather than built out of the red tufa. They were constructed at the end of the twelfth or the beginning of the thirteenth century by King Lalibela.

It is Christmas eve. Two oil lamps cast their light on the priests and cantors *(debteras)* as they sing the psalms surrounded by a group of the faithful. "Workeye, what does Christmas mean to you?" "It is the day of Christ's birth. I love Christ, he died for me. I love Mary too, she forgives my sins."

There are some drops of rain, and we take shelter in a corner. Workeye wraps himself up in his *shamma*, a cloak by day, a blanket by night. His Christmas eve meal? *Injira*, a sort of pancake made of a local grain, called *tef,* with a pimento sauce, called *wat*, thickened with lentils or beans. This is the daily fare of the Ethiopians; the rich add some meat to it.

The day before, Workeye fasted until noon. Monastic asceticism has left a deep mark on the spiritual life of Ethiopia. The ordinary faithful observe about one hundred eighty fast days a year; the priests keep two hundred fifty. His fast did not prevent Workeye from climbing like a mountain goat as he brought me to the church we were going to visit. He is used to suffering and effort: to get to his school, which is in the capital city of the province, he has to walk for three days along treacherous roads.

A priest comes up to us and shouts at Workeye. No translation needed; I know he wants money. The clergy do not take it lightly when the boys of Lalibela guide tourists, for this means that the boys gather in some of the manna the priests think ought to go to them. We go by an underground passage to another church. According to custom, Workeye takes off his sandals before entering. Did not God say to Moses, "Take the sandals off your feet because the ground on which you are standing is holy"? Many Christians, moreover, consider themselves unworthy to enter a church. They are content to prostrate themselves before the building and kiss its walls. Ethiopian theology puts the accent on the transcendence of God, who is eternal and omnipotent. In his presence, humans feel themselves to be essentially sinful and impure.

The liturgy lasts the whole night. Then, as the sun appears over the mountain, all the clergy of Lalibela and its surroundings line up along the wall of the church of St. Mary. Plaques depicting the nativity, St. Gabriel, St. Michael conquering the dragon, are brought out from the various sanctuaries. The priests are protected by multicolored parasols. Vested in white, with red sashes and turbans, the *debteras* hold timbrels in their hands and staffs on which they lean during the long hours of prayer.

There are about two hundred clergymen in the courtyard of the church and the crowd is on a slope at their backs. Seven or eight yards lower down the slope, a choir prepares to respond to the *debteras*. Then the drums resound, the timbrels are raised and lowered, and a ghostly, hoarse chant fills the whole courtyard, reaching right to the marrow of your bones, and lifting your soul. The *debteras* dance, or rather sway, to the rhythm of the music. It is a simple chant, but powerful and enthralling. Its origins go back to the beginning of the ages.

•

Abuna Aragaoui wanted to be a monk on this mountain impossible of access. He prayed to the Lord to help him live in solitude. During the night a serpent came down the mountain, took him by the belt, and lifted him up to the top.

Such is the legend about the founding of Debre Dammo, as a monk told it to me. That is the reason why we found ourselves at the foot of a smooth wall looking up at a door situated about one hundred fifty feet over our heads. A large rope hangs from the threshold of the door. You take hold of the rope and scale the wall, going up hand over hand. To stay faithful to the legend, the monks absolutely refuse to have a stairway built.

Abuna Aragaoui was one of the Nine Saints—undoubtedly Syrians—who came to Ethiopia toward the end of the fifth century and contributed greatly to the renewal of the spiritual life of the country at a time when faith was growing weak. They built many monasteries, two of which still exist in the Tigre region: Debre Dammo and Debre Libanos.

Debre Dammo is built on an *amba*, a tabletop mountain. The monastery resembles the villages of the region with small, stone houses and low walls forming an interior courtyard, pools of brackish water in the hollows of the rocks, and a few grazing oxen. There are no cows, nor are there ewes or she-goats: all female animals are forbidden. It is said that even the mosquitoes respect the interdict.

The monk is primarily one who has died to the world. When he makes profession, the burial rites are performed just as though he had physically died. It is true that he does not live on in descendants. Though an Ethiopian priest may marry, a monk takes a vow of celibacy: hence, the absence of anything feminine at the monastery.

Some monks become hermits. The White Father who took us to Debre Dammo once met one in a gorge. This man ate but a bit of corn, morning and evening. Stretched out on his cot, devoid of all clothing, he spent his time reciting the psalms. The priest asked him why he lived this way, and the hermit answered: "It is the world's medicine."

•

I wanted to begin this book with these sketches from Ethiopia (before the fall of Haile Selassie), first of all because they are still with me; secondly, because I had been so impressed with the culture and nobility of its people; and finally, because in this way I can begin to portray the universality of the church.

Do we not often forget that Jesus Christ was not born in the

West? (I once heard an old man recite the Our Father in Aramaic, the language in which it was first pronounced by our Lord Jesus. This was in the village of Maalula in Syria.) If the faith reached Rome quickly, it also spread in other directions, arriving, for example, about the year 330 in the kingdom of Axum, in what is today Ethiopia.

In the same way, long before St. Benedict, monasticism flourished in Egypt, Syria-Palestine, Asia Minor, and North Africa. The Ethiopian monastery of Debre Dammo is undoubtedly older than Monte Cassino, which was founded in the year 529 by St. Benedict.

It was thanks to colonialization that Christianity first arrived in many countries of Latin America, Africa, and Asia. But that age is past. I have no intention of putting that era, with all its shadows and highlights, on trial here. Pope John Paul II was to say at Lisieux: "What faith, what spiritual energy they had, those missionaries of the last century and the first half of this century!"

Rather than put the past on trial, it strikes me as more profitable to be present as the churches of the Third World emerge. Beyond any contribution from the West, they are attempting now, amid the pangs of childbirth, to bring their culture—its features that are unmoored by ours—into direct confrontation with the word of God.

The churches of the Third World (along with those of the "Fourth World" among us) are a privileged meeting place where the word of God and the poor come together. "The church wishes to be the church of the poor" (John Paul II, in Rio de Janeiro, July 2, 1980).

The West is no longer at the center of the Christian world. Important things are happening elsewhere. "I am convinced that the great age of Western theology has passed. . . . The Holy Spirit has left work for the Third World to do." This is how the Protestant theologian Ernst Käsemann expressed himself at the World Conference on Mission and Evangelization held by the World Council of Churches in May 1980, in Melbourne. At Kinshasa some African professors at the Catholic faculty of theology said to me: "Western theology must become one theology among many others and not the universal and exclusive theology of the church."

Assuredly, we have to avoid idealizing the situation. The churches of the Third World have some of the same ineptitudes and insufficiencies that we do. A missionary in Zambia once told me with a touch of humor: "This morning, in my struggle for the liberation of Africans, I spent one hour with a parishioner who wanted to know the name of the founder of the Legion of Mary, and whether or not he was canonized."

Nevertheless, the way that the young churches look upon revelation—from within a different culture and a context of poverty—the way they put it into practice, the way they live it, all this is a challenge to us. The gospel is a critique of every human society—including those that claim to be "revolutionary." The work of the Spirit among other Christians critiques our way of understanding the word of God and obeying it, our scale of values, our way of relating to creation, our economic priorities.

•

In the pages to follow you will read about those who live in slums, or those who have no place at all to live. No one is looking for your pity, still less for your money. The poor do not need our pity; they need our conversion. For a long time now, "foreign missions" meant sending out missionaries and supporting them with generous donations. That work is not finished; it is still necessary, even if now it is not exclusively a question of Europeans going out to the rest of the world: I have met Palestinian and Indian missionaries in Africa. Now we have not only to give but also to receive—and this is not easy. It is not a matter of accepting, in an attitude of condescension, the "contribution" of the Third World, of admitting that they have something valuable to offer us. We have to let ourselves be shaken up in our certitudes and changed in our outlook and behavior.

I have spent much of the past ten years visiting Christian communities in Africa, Asia, and Latin America. I was sent there by the Centre International de Reportages et d'Information Culturelle (CIRIC). A member of FIAC (Fédération Internationale

des Agences Catholiques), it specializes in sending research
teams (a journalist and a photographer) to compile reports on
the young churches in the Third World. This has been the origin
of the chapters to follow.   ˋ

This is not, then, a collection of systematic studies, but of
candid descriptions of what I have encountered on my journeys.
I make no pretense of giving a complete and exact picture of the
Third World. I write as a journalist, presenting straightforward
impressions of actual situations as I found them, without taking
into account their full historical background.

My wish is simply to pass on to the reader something of what
was confided to me—sometimes at great risk—by bishops,
priests, men and women religious, lay persons, and missionaries
whom I met on the way. I want to tell the reader what I have seen
and heard, most often marveling at what I found. I have only
one regret: that I have not understood or remembered everything, and that I am unable, except very imperfectly, to communicate what I have understood and remembered.

Part One

The Church:
Indigenous or Extraneous?

In many countries of Africa, Latin America, and Asia the gospel came with colonizers from the West. Western culture and the gospel message invaded those lands simultaneously. Missionaries—and it should surprise no one that they embraced the worldview of their contemporaries—propagated their civilization along with their faith. At times they looked upon the pagan world as "diabolical" and assaulted local religions in the name of the Truth.

Today Western culture continues to impose itself through the power of its economic superiority and the media of mass communication. This intrusion disrupts non-Western cultures. As Vincent Cosmáo has written, "condemned to identify themselves with someone else who is stronger and who assumes a mastery, persons who are thus dependent lose their own identity" *(Changer le monde, une tâche pour l'Eglise,* Paris: Cerf, 1979). They turn away from their own culture because it is not esteemed. On the contrary, "it is considered to be prescientific and superstitious. But they do not, for all that, have real access to the culture that has come to them from outside; they can

grasp it only superficially. They thus become alienated—
strangers to themselves. There is in the Third World a cultural
deprivation every bit as deplorable as the physical deprivation"
(ibid.).

Nevertheless, little by little, especially since Vatican II, the
church has appreciated more clearly the need "to understand
from the inside the beliefs and religious practices of the people
whom it goes out to meet" (ibid.). The church's message will be
understood only to the degree that "it takes hold, that it is assim-
ilated, interiorized, appropriated by the individuals or groups
whose culture it reinterprets without destroying" (ibid.). Fr.
Gerard Eschbach, a Dominican in Brazzaville, expressed it this
way: "The Christian outlook ought not to substitute itself for
African culture but rather challenge it to go beyond itself. We
need new fathers of the church." *African* fathers, of course.

At the outset, the peoples of Africa, Asia, and Latin America
received a Western incarnation of the faith. *Now* it is up to them
to incarnate Christ in their own culture. African theologians in
Kinshasa have said: "We will never have truly christianized our
people as long as we refer to our original beliefs in quotation
marks. The church must face these beliefs squarely."

This is not easy. But some progress has been made, and little
by little the face of the church of the Third World is beginning to
appear underneath the mask with which it had been disguised.
The liturgy is the place where this development is most visible.
At Kinshasa, I had the joy of participating in the Mass of Zaire
(Pope John Paul II let the opportunity pass by when he visited
there in the spring of 1980—which was deeply regretted by Cardinal Malula). What we see so far is only the beginning of a
process that will have to go on for many years. It may take us
much further than we think.

There is, of course, some resistance (the "intellectuals" of
Kinshasa demand that the Mass be in Latin), and there are difficulties: deciding what the cultural reference should be, in a milieu composed of many languages and tribes, remaining faithful
to a culture without clinging to a past that is no more ("we don't
need a church dressed in outdated clothes"), of relating to Christian communities already well westernized (Bombay, for example). And there are other problems. How can polygamy and the

African view of marriage be reconciled with the demands of the gospel? A study made in Ghana shows that 85 percent of the Catholics are excluded from the sacraments because their marital situation is irregular in the eyes of ecclesiastical law (*Informations Catholiques Internationales,* June 15, 1980).

Finally, the churches of the Third World, created in the image of the Western church and often weighed down with excessively heavy structures inherited from the past, depend all too often upon financial help from the West, particularly from the Vatican. This is hardly the best situation in which to assert one's individuality.

The church will never become truly catholic—universal—until all cultures contribute to it. Each culture is called to hear the word of God and to live under the impetus of the Holy Spirit. In this way it will make its own contribution to the building up of the kingdom of God.

Chapter 1

THE MADAGASCANS AND THEIR ANCESTORS

We are on one of the twelve hills that surround Antananarivo (formerly Tananarive). At its summit there is the tomb of a king. As is the yearly custom, the descendants and the former subjects of this king are assembled this morning near his tomb to sacrifice an ox. The fettered animal, struggling desperately, is led into the center of a circle formed by the crowd and is laid on its side. Toothless women dance all around it, in order to call down on the sacrifice the blessing of the ancestors.

A man plunges his lance into the neck of the ox. Someone removes the animal's heart and goes round the tomb several times before smearing its blood on a sacred stone. A witch doctor, dressed in white, pronounces a prayer addressed to Zahanary, the god of the Madagascans, and the crowd answers with a sort of amen.

As the ox is being cut up, a line forms in front of the witch doctor who sprinkles each person with water taken from a well also held to be sacred. The Madagascan friend who brought me points out to me the number of young persons in the line. "Despite Western culture, they still believe in the ancestors," she said to me. At that, someone standing near spoke out: "Everyone believes in ancestors!"

On the previous day I attended a *famadihana* in a village near the capital. Four beef cattle were slaughtered as well as two pigs

13

in order to feed those invited, and an orchestra was hired with clarinets, trumpets, and drums. A procession was formed with flag bearers leading the way. A half dozen persons, carrying on their shoulders an elongated bundle wrapped about with ribbons, were executing a dance step. They were followed by the crowd: men in straw hats, then the women, protected from the sun by parasols, and the children.

The bundle contained the mortal remains of a woman. They had been taken from the place where they had been temporarily laid a few months previously and were now being carried to their final resting place. When the cortege arrived at the family vault, new *lambas* (winding sheets of silk) were wrapped around the old ones. Then the minister said a prayer (it would have been a priest if the dead woman had been a Catholic), and a final hymn was chanted.

In addition to being a funeral ceremony, the *famadihana* is a feast in which one honors the ancestors and calls down their blessing. "The fact that we exhume their remains shows that we have not forgotten them." When the body has already been transferred, it suffices to go and change the *lambas*.

"For the Madagascan there is a bond between this world and the world beyond. In our villages the family tomb is close to the house: the worst of curses is to be banished from there. For then one is excluded from the community of the living and the dead. At every important undertaking in life, sacrifices are offered at the sacred place and we go to the tomb of our ancestors to ask their blessing."

My Madagascan friend is Christian. She sees no contradiction between her faith and the cult of ancestors: "On the contrary, it seems to me that we are quite within the Christian view of things when we show all this respect for the dead. It is the sign of our belief in the survival of the soul, and in the communion that exists between ourselves and those who are in the other world."

"For the Madagascan there is only one God, the creator and master of destiny. Every life obeys this unique Being. Nevertheless, this basic monotheism does not exclude intermediaries, and in particular one's ancestors. They are not gods—contrary to what some missionaries thought—but beings who continue to interest themselves in us from the other side of death." This is, in substance, how the Madagascan Jesuit, Fr. Francis Xavier Tabao, who has since become the bishop of Mananjary, explained to me the religious outlook of his people. It was a few months after the "cultural revolution" of May 1972. This movement, in addition to its social aspects (the revolt of the "little ones"), and its political designs (the overthrow of President Tsiranana), had as one of its goals to "madagascanize" Madagascar.

Fr. Tabao's attitude was: "I came from the ancestors and I will return to the ancestors." Madagascans sense that their existence is linked with that of the cosmos; they are at one with the universe. If they become isolated, they run the risk of losing their existence. The West has reduced the world to the domain of the visible. The European wants to be the subject of the forces of the cosmos; the Madagascan is more content to be their object.

Dissatisfied with the lack of ties with their ancestors, the invisible beings, the Catholic Madagascans tend toward a sort of syncretism. "Christianity could see only the work of the devil in the forces believed in by Madagascans. 'Paganism' is identified with Satan, when really it is a matter of a worldview that was only waiting for Christ."

God has been revealed to the Madagascan as the creator, but not as a father. "One finds oneself faced with an unknown 'mechanism' and thus one lives with a certain fear. Our life is spent in the effort to reestablish a balance between that 'mechanism' and ourselves." Hence the rites designed to reconcile oneself with the cosmos, and with one's ancestors.

•

"Christianity began as something from the West and not as something from among us," continued Fr. Tabao. He went on to tell me this story about his native village of Ankatafana, situated at the mouth of the Mananjary River.

"It was about 1930. Our parents went to speak to the administrator of Mananjary, the next village, to ask him for a school. The administrator sent them to the Catholic mission. The missionaries agreed to build a school, but they also wanted to build a church. They built a church in the style of a traditional hut, but the pillars were made of reinforced concrete. The pagans told them: 'You are going counter to our customs. This church will be leveled by our ancestors.' A cyclone came and the church was, in fact, destroyed. The missionaries were not discouraged, and this time they set themselves to build the whole church out of concrete. The pagans said: 'You are calling down a catastrophe on our village. This church too will be destroyed.' When work on the church began, the sea was about two or three hundred yards from the site. Then it began to eat away at the shore in the direction of the church and the village. The pagans told them: 'It is not that the sea is advancing, but rather that our ancestors are digging the sand with their shovels. They do not want a sanctuary dedicated to the ancestors of the whites, Jesus and Mary.' On the day the church was first used, the sea was only three yards away. Soon the church was swallowed by the sea and then the village suffered the same fate. The faith that had begun to take root in the area disappeared. People had proof that their ancestors had conquered the ancestors of the whites. Someone once said to a missionary, 'I am not a Christian, I am a Madagascan.' "

A Madagascan catechist was described to me by his parish priest in these terms: "By our standards he would be said to possess very limited theological equipage, but I can only admire his practical theology."

This same catechist told me the following: "Very few Madagascan elements have found their way into the Catholic religion. It is a European faith. People must instead study the customs of our country and see how they may be integrated into Christianity. Faith and the cult of our ancestors are not mutually exclusive. A French priest was struck by this remark by one of his flock: 'Madagascan customs are bad; European customs are good.' He then realized that people had been forced to become westernized in order to become Christian."

The "imported" character of the faith is accentuated by material dependence. "We live on alms and aid from the Vatican. Christians are thus maintained in a status of being on relief." As a European bishop put it: "There is too much proselytizing based on handouts." (In South Korea I heard talk of "rice Christians," those who became Christian when they received help in the form of food.)

At the same time, a whole infrastructure—buildings, and so forth—was erected that does not fit the Madagascan church (or other churches of the Third World). "What we have been given is too heavy for us. The beautiful churches clash with the huts of the peasants. We used to be proud of these churches and we felt that we had to keep up with the Protestants. Now, we have to take up the task of evangelization at the level of the people, with modest means." This is how a Madagascan priest expressed it to me.

No one is throwing stones at the previous generation of missionaries ("we probably wouldn't have done any better than they did"), but now Christianity must be preached in a new way. Account must be taken of the new awareness ushered in by the events of 1972, but initiated long before that. To name but one of the many problems: Madagascan priests were trained as were Westerners. "They are cut off from the mass of the people, the simple landworkers; they are more at ease in the city, in a ministry of sacramentalization, than out in the back woods." (Along the same lines, this is what I heard in Zambia: "For a certain number of African priests, especially among the older clergy, accession to the priesthood represented a great step upward on the social scale. Now they want nothing to change. They wear the Roman collar and cling to all the symbols of their position. At first, they were opposed to having African music in the liturgy. They felt humiliated and said to us: 'You think that we are incapable of singing Gregorian chant.' " In Tanzania some seminarians said: "The missionaries who came from Europe could not live as we do. They constructed their kind of buildings and educated African priests as if they were Europeans.")

The missionary effort began with baptizing and building. A great number of schools were built in order to achieve the greatest number of conversions. Now faith must be deepened, and the Madagascan face of the church must be discovered.

Chapter 2

THE CONGO: DECOLONIZATION OF RELIGION

We are at the Le Briz station on the Congo-Ocean railroad line. About two miles higher up is the Benedictine monastery of La Bouenza, just beside the transformer station that relays electricity from the dam built by the Chinese. The community numbers seven Frenchmen and seven Africans (six from the Congo Republic and one from the Cameroons). In addition, there are students from other African monasteries who come for a one-year training course.

As to the physical layout: there are a number of buildings scattered about an area planted with palm trees, bougainvillea, and bamboo. As to external activity: there are facilities for retreats, a dispensary (one of the French monks is a physician), a small workshop where medicaments are made, and a farm for raising beef cattle and pigs. The essence of the life is, of course, "a life totally consecrated to the Lord," as Bro. John, of the Congolese, soon to be ordained a priest, expressed it to me. He went on to add, "The African is a person of prayer; that is not something that was imported."

What was brought to Africa was the Rule of St. Benedict. However, it is obvious today that such a rule cannot simply be "exported" and applied without modification to the African situation. Fr. Sergius, the prior, said to me: "We are not seeking to discover what French monastic life might be, but rather what the monastic life itself is. The essence cannot change, but as for the rest, it must be adapted to the African temperament. We have already come a long way in this regard."

An example of such adaptation is the rule of silence. Africans experience a need to live in contact with others and this contact has to be expressed by words and gestures. "That is why we decided a short time ago to speak during breakfast. In that way the day begins in an atmosphere of brotherly communication, and that is good for the community."

In the same way, the principles operative in Europe regarding the relationship between the monk and his family cannot be transposed to an African milieu. "To cut an African monk off from his family and his ancestors is unthinkable. He would fall sick; it would be a kind of death for him." If a problem arises in the monk's family, it is absolutely necessary that he go back to his village. "At first we had difficulty acknowledging this," admitted the prior.

Furthermore, though in Europe families are usually in a position to help the monks, in Africa it is the monks who must come to the aid of their families. Every Congolese who has completed his studies must reimburse his family. "The monastery must aid the families of the monks. For them, true poverty consists in not being able to maintain their parents in the lifestyle they would wish."

Another French monk, Fr. Bede, regrets that the modifications of the rule seem to have been "extorted," so to speak. "We are obliged to tolerate cetain adjustments, but really, there should be no question of 'tolerating' anything. We must, rather, conceive of monastic life differently, build something new without regret or a backward glance. The ideal is not elsewhere—and out of reach. The ideal is an African community."

This is surely not to take the easy way. How is it possible to form an African community, a Congolese community, above tribal and linguistic divisions? On what cultural bases would it be built? Fr. Bede stressed the fact that the majority of Africans in the Bouenza region had lost touch with the deep meaning of their own customs. As for the Congolese who have grown up in the large cities, most of them understand but poorly their African culture though they remain permeated by it. Fr. Bede's answer was: "We must insist first and foremost on the gospel, and create an original and authentic religious life that takes its birth from the word of God."

The questions being faced by the monastery of Bouenza are those that confront the whole of the Congolese church. I remember a layman in Brazzaville who told me: "Even if there have been some small changes in the liturgy, the church remains European. It is not yet *our* church. I have always thought that we should be decolonized religiously as well as politically. When the missionaries came here, we were not a *tabula rasa*: we had our religious traditions. We must restore them and use them as our point of departure." (In Tanzania someone said to me: "We are independent politically, but not economically or religiously.")

•

Now we are in Kinshasa, on the other side of the Congo (or Zaire) River. It is the parish of St. Alphonsus in the lower-class quarter of town, Matete, Sunday evening, six o'clock. The church is full; there are perhaps two thousand persons present. Everyone is singing, led by the choir and accompanied by tom-toms, an electric guitar, and two accordions. The sound fills the air: I have never heard a crowd sing with such feeling. Led by acolytes and readers, all adults, the priest advances up the central aisle with a dancing movement.

The Mass—an ordinary Sunday Mass—will last two hours. During those two hours I will be lifted up by the fervor of the prayer of this community, I will be overwhelmed by the beauty of the celebration, and electrified by a sense of communion that is almost palpable. But do not imagine some sort of wild exaltation! Rather, it is an intense joy, the existential joy that lives in Africans, and finds expressions in rhythm, music, and color.

The Roman rite has, in some ways, been rethought by the Africans who, while guarding the essentials, have transposed it into their own culture, their own thought patterns. The result is the Mass of Zaire, which was born right here in the parish of St. Alphonsus. It was a Zairian liturgist, Fr. Mpongo, who gave form to the ideas that came from the people of Kinshasa. He explained certain aspects of this Mass to me: "We put ourselves in the presence of the other world when we invoke the saints and ancestors. We address God along with them. The penance ceremony takes place after the readings: our life is judged by the word of God. Having acknowledged our sins, we must be reconciled with the Lord and with others. The offertory is the handing back of the gifts that seal our peace and communion, the meal that we share when friendship is once again restored. The priest represents Christ—the head of the church. That is why he carries a staff of authority in his hand and is surrounded by lance bearers. The striped colors of the liturgical robes are the sign of the diversity of this earth, which must be put in communication with the world beyond. There is always a cosmic character to our celebrations."

What has been done so far is but one stage. There are improvements to be made in the Mass of Zaire, and no one knows exactly what the final form will be. I asked Cardinal Malula, archbishop of Kinshasa, if the direction was toward an African rite that would be as different from ours as is an Oriental rite. The substance of his reply was: "It is easy for me to say yes, and my answer is justifiable. Nevertheless, there are many obstacles, especially on the part of the West, which has difficulty in admitting that every church, united in the same faith and in union with the Holy See, may have its own rite. The fact that Africa too follows the Roman rite is due to historical accident. If we had been colonized by Orientals, what rite would we have now? But a historical accident is not an absolute, and it can be changed. We are, however, up against the cultural imperialism of the West."

Chapter 3

THE PERUVIAN ANDES: WHAT DO THEY REALLY BELIEVE?

We have cleared the Ocepuno Pass, more than fifteen thousand feet above sea level, and we pause between a Christian cross and an Inca monument that face each other, standing guard on either side of the dirt road. The car descends into a valley dominated by snow-capped peaks: Allincapac ("the rich lord"), and Chichicapac ("the evil lord"), rising up about twenty thousand feet. We are facing great, silent spaces where only flocks of llamas and alpacas live.

The road soon enters a gorge which, about sixty miles farther down, converges with the Amazon forest. We get out of the car and descend a path that takes us to the bank of the river San Gaban. We walk over a bridge and follow a path barely traceable among the fallen boulders; it leads up a steep incline. Our hearts are pounding. This is the only way to reach Tantamaco.

After about an hour we see the first houses, stone with thatched roofs. They are hardly distinguishable from the scattered rocks and low walls of the paddocks. Beyond that, thin fields cling to the shadowed mountain overlooking the village. The mountain seems to resent having to tolerate the presence of human beings here, a discreet presence at that, barely perceptible amid this great and pitiless land of stone.

We enter by a narrow alley onto the village square before a charming church flanked by two square towers. There are about a dozen vendors with their wares sheltered under tents and, at each corner of the square, a bouquet of Peruvian flags. It is a festival day at Tantamaco. Villagers lead the priest whom we are accompanying, a Swiss missionary (Fidei Donum), Xavier Arbex, up to the *alferado*. There can be no celebration without one or several *alferados* who organize the festivities and bear the expense in return for a special blessing and a good measure of prestige.

There is a table set: we are served cheese, potatoes (tiny at this altitude), meat, and onions. This, along with wool, is just about all that Tantamaco produces. What else could you ask of Pachamama ("mother earth") when you live two and a half miles up, closer to heaven than to the fertile valleys below?

Candles are distributed and a procession marches to the church just as night falls on the mountains around us. Large shadows climb up the bare walls and lose themselves in the thatching of the roofs. I am gripped by the piercing cold, and gripped as well by the austere beauty of the chapel with no chairs or pews. Men, woman, and children, all copper-colored with eyes like burning embers, stand wrapped in their ponchos. I look at those enigmatic faces, faces from another world.

"We have begun to realize that we are talking to a world about which we know nothing, and which we can hardly enter. They are Christians as we are. They perform the same rites we do (they tend to do more). And yet it is obvious that they are from another culture, another civilization, another world; that they live deeply (too deeply?) within themselves. It is a conquered civilization, one that seems distant yet hostile at the same time; there is something in them that has been brooding for centuries."

They are Christians but they belong to another religion as well, that of Pachamama, for which the Incas were unable to substitute their own cult of the sun, and which the Spanish were never able to eradicate from their soul. To this day, before they begin to work a field, they make an offering of cocoa beans and wine to appease the land they are about to wound.

Bishop Dalle, a Frenchman, thinks that "in each of these persons there coexist zones that are Christian and others that are pre-Inca." It is a syncretism that does not seem to give rise to unbearable tensions. "Their way of thinking is different from ours: they do not know about the principle of contradiction." One truth does not necessarily exclude another and the two systems of belief can exist side by side without ever coming into conflict.

"Nevertheless, we can see that they don't believe in the same way we do."

"What do they believe?"

"I'd really like to know."

They are all baptized, but just how far has the Christianity of the Spanish colonizers penetrated their soul? Blessings, processions, the cult of the dead all play an essential part in their religion. There is a strong accent on the cross—a characteristic of Spanish piety—and this corresponds to the mentality of the people and to their suffering. On the other hand, they never get married in the church, and the eucharist inspires only a reverential (or superstitious?) fear.

On the village square a punch (hot milk, alcohol, sugar, and cinnamon) is being served by the light of oil lamps. Out of the cold night comes the village band of Tantamaco: a drum, cymbals, and eerie panpipes. Villagers begin to dance to a light rhythm and they bring the *padrecito* (their affectionate term for the priest) into the circle.

●

It is now Sunday morning. The sunlight is falling straight down on the village. Two chickens cross the square between the vendors' tents with small piles of candies, candles, beer, canned tuna, and cookies. There is a variety shop whose proprietor plays his radio loud as he hawks aspirins, necklaces, kitchen knives, cigarettes, and toys. The consumer society has invaded Tantamaco.

The band returns. Eyes half closed, and with uncertain steps, the musicians mount the road that leads to the church. They had played until five in the morning at the house of the *alferado* where the dancers had taken refuge from the cold. The cocoa had made them forget their fatigue, and the alcohol had kept

them warm, but now they are just about done in. Another band,
this one having some powerful brass instruments, will soon
come and drown out the cries of the panpipes.

The *padrecito* gathers the community and addresses them:
"Some of you are criticizing Alejandro the catechist. I am not
going to celebrate Mass until this affair has been cleared up. I
only want to say that the catechists receive no advantage from
their functions. The only thing they are given is their food when
they come to meetings."

A long discussion ensues. Everybody thinks that the gringo
priests are rich and give big handouts to those who work with
them. From this comes jealousy. I was told: "It used to be that
the catechist was a sort of intermediary: the priest tried to teach
doctrine to him so that he could pass it on to his village. Now,
the ideal is that the catechist become a leader in his community."
This is absolutely necessary if the hope of finally seeing an indigenous church in the Andes is to be realized. It has been more
than four centuries since the first missionaries came here and we
still can do no better than to go to Geneva, Paris, or Madrid and
find a priest to come and say Mass here!

Two-thirds of the priests working in Peru are from outside the
country. And those who are Peruvian citizens are not necessarily
any closer to the Andean world: "Even if they were born in the
heart of this world, they are taken and put in a seminary where
professors talk to them about Thomas Aquinas, Voltaire, Marx,
and Marcuse. They finish up being as much outsiders as we are."

Alejandro and his critics are reconciled. Mass can begin. Despite all the efforts on the part of the *padrecito* to make the Mass
comprehensible, it does not "go" well. At the end of the Mass
the men hoist a float onto their shoulders. It is decorated with
blond chubby angels and bears a statue of St. Isidore, the patron
of the village. They process around the square, stopping at each
corner to pray before an oratory. Firecrackers are set off. It is a
festival day at Tantamaco. . . .

Chapter 4

THAILAND: FACE TO FACE
WITH BUDDHISM

The freshness of the dawn air tingles your nostrils. One
after another, five pairs of bare feet silently tread on the sand
path. As you raise your eyes you see saffron robes and then
shaven heads. The monks, each with their own bowl the size of a
large pot, are starting out to get their daily rice from the villages
near their monastery.

A woman is kneeling back on her heels with an infant clinging
to her. In her hands there is a basket that she holds out as if making an offering. As the first monk reaches her and uncovers his
bowl, she puts in a handful of rice. She repeats this gesture for
the four others. She gets up when they have passed on. No one
said a word—neither the monks nor the woman nor the infant;
their eyes never met.

The monks continue to file through the village more solemnly
than in a cathedral. In front of the wooden houses on piles,
which seemed hunched over amid the leafy branches of banana
and palm trees, are other women, other infants, and some men
as well. They are kneeling or standing; one shivers, another
yawns, their eyes are still moist with sleep. They put a handful of
rice in the bowls, wait until the saffron robes have disappeared
and then go inside. The day can begin.

For more than an hour—though time seemed suspended—I
followed the Buddhist monks, being careful not to bother them.

26

Their quest for rice had no air of begging about it; it was more like a beautiful and austere liturgy.

We enter the enclosure of the monastery, the *wat,* Nong Pa Pong. At first there is a forest of leaves, then a series of buildings, not very many, set in a vast clearing. With measured pace, other groups are also returning from their morning rounds. There are about forty monks in all, and they assemble in a long room with large, low tables against the walls. Each one takes his place seated on the floor in a semi-lotus position: legs crossed, torso upright.

In order of seniority, they begin to eat, bending over their bowls and making small balls of rice with their fingers (there may also be peices of fish, vegetables, and fruit all mixed together in the rice). They put the food in their mouths and chew it slowly, their gazes averted. It would never occur to anyone to speak to them: they are as absent as if they were a hundred miles away.

As well as being a meal, the only one of the day, this is a time of meditation. One pays absolute attention to what one is doing. "Nothing should be done mechanically, but always with full awareness, in full possession of one's psychological forces. One eats without passion, with detachment. It is a question of avoiding physical desires, animality. Physical sensations are neither denied nor refused—it is not forbidden to find good things good—but one must never be dominated by sensation."

When the meal is over, each one carefully cleans his bowl with water and leaves. Nothing is left for the next day. The monks live on what is given them each day by their neighbors. Each monk now retires to his *kuti,* a tiny hut isolated in the forest. It is there that he passes the greater part of his time, walking in front of his dwelling or remaining immobile within it.

When I visited, there were a dozen guest monks at the Nong Pa Pong monastery, which is in the northeast of Thailand. They were, no doubt, attracted there by the reputation for holiness of the founder of the monastery. He had spent twenty-five years as a wandering monk in the forest before he was offered this retreat by the local villagers. He was then joined by disciples. There was also at the *wat* a Catholic priest, Fr. Edmond Pezet, and I went to see him in his *kuti.*

"When I came here, I made it clear to the Master that I would remain a Christian. There was no question of my becoming a Buddhist like the other Europeans and Americans who live here."

Fr. Pezet had been three months at the monastery, submitting to all the rules of the monastery (there are 227 of them). He had his head shaven and wore a white robe, as a postulant, instead of a saffron robe. He had added a small table and stool to the "furnishings" of the *kuti,* which was made entirely of mats.

"When I first came to Thailand in 1956, I was struck by the fact that I had come to a country that was Buddhist. For a long time Buddhism had been considered simply an obstacle to evangelization, but many missionaries began to have an uneasy conscience about this view."

For generations a great effort had been made to protect Christians from any contact with the pagoda. The faithful were forbidden to participate in any Buddhist ceremony, even if it was the marriage or funeral of a relative, under pain of a "reserved sin." An ordinary confession would not suffice; only the bishop could absolve one from such a fault, and often a public asking of pardon was required.

It is easy to imagine that all this resulted in adamantine prejudices and mutual ignorance. Buddhists had no trouble looking upon Christianity as a variety of animism, and Christians considered themselves superior to Buddhists. Fr. Pezet resolved to do what he could to break down these barriers. Because of parish duties he had to wait until 1970 before he could begin his project. The first step was to study Buddhism from books.

"What I am doing now in the *wat* is different. The Master doesn't care much for book study. He puts the accent on practice. The only way to know Buddhism is by practicing it."

As we were talking, a magnificent grouse came up to us without any fear. The monks maintain an absolute nonviolence. They must even spare the mosquitoes, and there are many of them in these woods. . . .

"I make no attempt to bring anything to the Buddhists," Fr. Pezet continued. "If they want to receive something from me, that is for them to do. My goal is to reveal Buddhism to Christians. If there had never been a Vatican Council II, I could not do what I am doing; it wouldn't be accepted. Even now it isn't easy."

I found this to be true enough. A Thai priest told me, "What Fr. Pezet is trying may be good for him personally, but I don't see how it can bear any fruit for the church." And a missionary remarked: "The indigenous clergy has received a completely occidental training along with the faith. They don't know how to sort it out, and they are afraid of losing something that may be important."

Nevertheless, there is a new awareness beginning. It is no longer rare for Christians to try some various approaches to Buddhism. For many, this means first of all acquiring a theoretical knowledge, particularly in conferences, which Fr. Pezet often participates in. Courses in meditation are being given by Buddhist monks in the Jesuit house at Bangkok. A Thai priest said this to me: "The church has remained a stranger here, and we are looked upon as strangers by our Buddhist compatriots. We have to change, to incarnate our faith with the values of the country, to modify the way we live. . . ."

Catholics make up less than 0.5 percent of the population of Thailand. Many of them are of Chinese or Vietnamese origin, which adds to the impression that Christians are strangers. It is not easy for a minority to affirm its identity in the eyes of a majority opposed to it, without at the same time stressing all the ways that it is different. "It is not easy to discern what belongs to the culture of Thailand and what belongs to the Buddhist or animistic tradition," said the archbishop of Bangkok. Nevertheless, either the church will become Thai or it will cease to exist in Thailand.

Chapter 5

TUNISIA: ALLAH AKBAR!

We are in front of the mosque in Gafsa, the morning of *Aid el Kebir,* the "Great Feast." Inside the mosque the faithful are crying out *Allah Akbar!* ("Allah is great!"). Children are playing outside in the vast courtyard in the sunlight. We stand at the threshold uniting our prayer with that of the men inside, who have their backs to us, and of the few old women who are at the back of the hall.

The imam had invited us. "You may take pictures if you do it discreetly, so that the worshipers feel that they are being respected. We have nothing to hide. We go to the mosque to adore God, and that is an honorable thing."

We had visited the imam the day before, accompanied by his friend Fr. Maurice Garau, a diocesan priest born in Tunisia who works now as a male nurse in the Gafsa hospital. The imam, an old man with a handsome, deeply etched face, and slow of movement, was performing the ablutions before going to prayer: "Cleanliness of body is a sign of purity of heart." And then he added by way of welcome: "They who understand Islam know that it carries a spirit of brotherhood between peoples, races, and tribes. If everyone followed religious principles, there would be no war, but rather universal cooperation." He then recited once again those verses of the Koran that state that Christians are those closest to Moslems, and turned to Fr. Garau: "Monsieur Garau is my brother; my house is his house."

He left us then, to go to lead the prayers. When he returned, as we were drinking coffee, I asked him to explain the meaning of the Great Feast, during which the many sheep I had seen tied up before the houses would be immolated.

"We are recalling the sacrifice of Abraham when God told him to sacrifice his son Ishmael." He opened up a well used copy of the Koran and read out for us the dialogue between Abraham and Ishmael: Abraham tells Ishmael of his coming death, and the boy responds, "O father, do what you have been commanded." Then, following a Moslem tradition, the imam told us the story: "Ishmael said to Abraham, 'I am more worthy than you, because I am making a gift of my life.' But Abraham replied, 'No, it is I who am more worthy because I am sacrificing more than my life.' Then God intervened, 'I am even more worthy and more generous than both of you. I am providing a ram to be sacrificed in place of Ishmael.' "

At the thought of the goodness of God, tears filled the eyes of the imam and his voice cracked. Then he added: "God has overwhelmed us with his generosity. May he be exalted! How great is God!"

Later, with a white veil covering his head, the imam rose up to preach, at the far end of the mosque. His sermon, which recounted the story of Abraham and Ishmael, was punctuated by the cries of the faithful: *Allah Akbar!*

Fr. Garau said to us: "The imam is always very moved when he speaks like this. He has a deep sense of the greatness of God and of his own unworthiness to be preaching the divine word." Just then a woman came out of the mosque, and Fr. Garau said to her: "May God hear your prayer!" She responded: "May God hear the prayer of each one of us!"

Fr. Garau had come to the oasis of Gafsa ten years earlier. It is the gateway to the desert, whose ochre, blue, and white colors shimmer in the sunlight. He had just received his diploma as a nurse and the Tunisian Ministry of Health sent him to this tiny village. Since that time he has been the leader of the small local Christian communities—composed of non-Tunisians—and has lived in friendship with the Moslems around him, and worked as a nurse.

"The hospital is a special place to meet others. The sick are extremely sensitive to any act of kindness or attention. They call me Abderrahmam, the 'servant of the Merciful One.' As a hospital employee, you come to know a great number of persons. I never get on a bus without coming across someone whom I have either taken care of personally or whose family I have treated."

One of Fr. Garau's first visits was to the imam Ali Mehrez, the leader of the mosque. "That visit began a friendship. It grew slowly; it is important to take time. Little by little, over the months and years we were able to get to know one another deeply. Today, there is a perfect confidence between us; there are no shadows. We support one another in our pilgrimage as believers. For me, meeting with this imam is like meeting with a priest. We commune in God."

I asked Fr. Garau what Islam had given to him. "I am struck by the sense that Moslems have of the transcendence and greatness of God, and by their rejection of all the idols of our modern world. Then too, they possess, in a deep and spontaneous way, a sense of hospitality and generosity."

Fr. Garau considers himself to be a witness of what the Spirit accomplishes in human hearts, including those of non-Christians: "Just as certain individuals are called to the work of biblical exegesis, so I am called to read the life of Jesus Christ in the life of other persons, particularly in the lives of the Moslems among whom I am immersed. I want to be a mystical explorer. It is fascinating, isn't it? It is not very interesting to go someplace to discover the work of the devil, but it is fascinating to find—in all clarity—the marvels of God and to communicate them to the church in speech or writing."

Part Two

New Communities,
New Ministries

On the island of Mindanao, in the Philippines, I learned of parishes that had two priests for seventy thousand persons. In Santiago, Chile, there is a priest who, alone, must look after three parishes comprising fifty thousand persons. I spent some days in the Congo in a parish whose territory extended thirty-one miles in length. I discovered all these things though I was in no way looking for exceptional cases.

If the church wants to provide even a minimal presence, it cannot be content with traditional structures: a large building for worship, a convent, a school, or a hospital. For some years now various types of local communities have been growing. Everyone knows about the basic communities in Brazil and elsewhere in Latin America, and their equivalent is found in Africa and Asia (and Europe as well).

The existence of these communities implies the existence of new types of ministry. There is an almost endless variety of them. Ministers may be women religious, deacons, married persons, men or women, young persons. They may work alone or as part of a team, a committee, a diocesan office. They can be chosen by the parish priest or by the community. They may be called *kaabag* (in Mindanao), *mokambi* (in Kinshasa), minister of the word (in Chile or Nicaragua), catechist, presiding elder, leader, or whatever.

Very often, the church is most alive in these new communities. Very often too, it is upon these new ministries that the hope rests for a renewed Christianity, in contact with daily life, and concerned to reach others. Often these communities evidence examples of sacrifice, gift of self, and even of heroism and undeniable sanctity.

One question arises again and again in regard to those exercising new ministries: could they be ordained and celebrate the eucharist in their community? It is often pointed out that to say Mass is easier than to preach, and many of the men in these new ministries are already preaching. The proposal, however, meets with some objections. Some are afraid, for instance, that it could result in a "second-class clergy," on the presumption that the university-level education given to the "first-class clergy" is the best possible kind of training. Others point to the problem of celibacy.

As a discipline of the Latin church (I have met married priests among the Lebanese Maronites and the Greek Catholics, in union with Rome), ecclesiastical celibacy does not always correspond to the culture or the de facto situation of priests in Africa or Latin America, where celibacy is not held in universal respect.

In the following pages, you will meet a *mokambi* from Zaire. This is what he had to say on this subject: "At the beginning we were all laymen. When I committed myself to this work I never had the idea of becoming a priest, and I still don't. Nevertheless, if church authorities decide one day that we should be ordained, we could not refuse it."

In the Congo, Fr. Portella, vicar general of the diocese of Pointe-Noire, told me that at the moment there is no question of ordaining the married men who are leaders of the *mabundu* ("community"). "Such decisions need a long time to mature. To set useful directions for the future requires that we first understand the full import of the tradition we have received. We have to go through a whole process of critical analysis regarding this tradition and to make our own judgments on it before we can take our distance from it. Let us take the time to bring about the necessary changes in keeping with our way of doing things and at our own rhythm."

Even as we wait, we can see in the Third World a remarkable flourishing of ministries, mostly undertaken by lay persons, as in the early days of the church.

Chapter 6

KINSHASA: LAY PASTORS

We are being called together by a chant. It serves the function of church bells. We walk down a sandy street in this section of Ngaba, which spreads out on a gentle slope stretching down to the river on the outskirts of Kinshasa. Night falls on the small tin-roofed houses under the palm trees. The vendors—of peanuts, manioc flour, cigarettes, dried fish, soap—light their oil lamps.

We come to an open area where two hundred persons, children included, are gathered around a table decorated with two artificial flowers, a candle, and a crucifix. "*Batata, bamama, bilenge, mbote!*" "*Mbote!*" The leader of the group, a craftsman by trade, greets the fathers and mothers without leaving out the children *(bilenge)*. He is opening the weekly meeting of the base community of Mpiko. He reads a passage of the gospel (the choosing of the twelve apostles) and a discussion ensues. It is the beginning of the dry season; the night is fresh while the moon looks down through a half-closed eye.

"Yes, Jesus has chosen us as well, we are apostles. We must stand by all those who suffer, to help them, to share their difficulties, to pray with them. This is our task as lay Christians."

The Christians are encouraged to approach non-Christians in order to bring them to the catechetical program for adults. Then, a misunderstanding about the sacrament of the sick must be cleared up. Many are afraid that when the priest comes it is to take hold of the spirit of a dying person. "No, it is just to

36

strengthen the faith of the person about to leave us."

There is another song and then the neighborhood news: a house has burned down, the wife of one of the members of the community is sick, a baby has been born, a widow has urgent need of assistance. . . .

•

This Wednesday night, as on every Wednesday, nine base communities are meeting at the parish of St. Lawrence. They make up but a minority of the faithful: four hundred fifty adults in all, out of the twelve or thirteen thousand Catholics in the territory served by St. Lawrence. But this type of community is spreading throughout the capital of Zaire.

"We have changed our methods of evangelization," Cardinal Malula, the archbishop of Kinshasa, told me. "Rather than start with the parish, we begin with entities that are smaller, of a more human dimension."

Help for the poor and suffering, funeral ceremonies—so important in Africa—the catechizing of children, all take place at the level of the base community. It is here, too, that all the hundreds of problems of daily life are discussed and entered into: helping a couple about to break up, replacing a roof blown away by the wind, cleaning the gutters. . . . Without denying the importance of prayer, members are trying to go beyond the stage of meeting *only* for prayer.

Just as the meeting was about to adjourn, a man stood up. He was very thin, with burning eyes set in an emaciated face. He expressed once again the role of the communities: "We want to bring the gospel into our section of the city. Our faith should be making a different life right there where we live."

The man who spoke thus is the *mokambi* of St. Lawrence. The father of six children, from ages two to fifteen, he is a teacher by profession. At the same time he is leader of the parish; you would call him the pastor if the title were not reserved for priests.

The first *bakambi* (the plural form of *mokambi*: "guide") were officially installed in 1975. By 1978 eleven of the sixty parishes had been confided to their care. The system began almost by chance. "A missionary was appointed to a newly developing area of the capital and religious activities began. But then he was called to do something else and had to leave that place. Still, the community could not be left to itself, with him coming only on Sundays for Mass. So, the missionary got the idea of asking a layman, who had just completed two years of training at the Institute for Religious Studies, to take responsibility for the nascent parish."

Cardinal Malula gave official standing to the experiment. He told me: "We wanted to involve the laity as fully as possible in the work of evangelization. In times past, the priest took upon himself many tasks that were not necessarily sacerdotal, and by that fact alone he had a say in everything, while the lay person's role was reduced to that of listening. We know, however, from the theology of baptism and confirmation that every Christian is sent by the Lord to spread the faith."

The primary reason that set the church of Kinshasa in this direction, said the cardinal, was not the shortage of priests but the desire to accord to lay persons their rightful place. It remains true, nevertheless, that the population of Zaire's capital grows each year by about one hundred or one hundred fifty thousand, and the presence of *bakambi* allows new parishes to be opened even though there are not priests available.

In addition, this move favors the africanization of the church in a diocese where the priests of local origin engaged in parish work can be counted on the fingers of one hand. "In this regard we were behind the Protestants," remarked Fr. Daniel Delanote, a Belgian, and pioneer of the *mokambi* innovation.

•

I met many *bakambi*, but it was with the *mokambi* of St. Lawrence, Citizen Mongu Ekongo that I spent the most time. (The Mobutu government has banned the title *Monsieur* ["Mr."] and *Madame* ["Mrs."], as well as Christian first names, in the interest of African "authenticity.") I have the greatest respect for this layman, who gives himself unstintingly to a task from which he derives no material advantage, except a place to live. In fact, none of the *bakambi* receive any remuneration for their church-related work.

This is how Citizen Mongu Ekongo spends his time. Each morning, from seven-thirty to twelve-thirty, is devoted to his profession as a teacher. The afternoon, evenings, and Sundays are given to the parish. On Tuesdays, Thursdays, and Fridays the *mokambi* receives the faithful in his office. They bring to him their problems, of the neighborhood or the family, and ask his advice or help. On the other days of the week, there are training sessions for the leaders of the base communities and those responsible for catechesis or other activities. The *mokambi* must also visit the poor and the sick, find ways to finance the parish (with help from the finance committee), prepare his homilies, and so forth.

"My mind is always occupied either with the school or with my ministry. I have no time for leisure. I derive my courage and my joy from seeing the parish grow. Seven years ago there were eight of us; now the church is full every Sunday. There are about one hundred lay persons in positions of responsibility, and the Spirit is at work among us. All this gives me joy."

As Fr. Allary, a Belgian Jesuit who is the "priest leader" of St. Lawrence, recognized, "the task of a *mokambi* demands heroism." He added: "Mongu Ekongo is a man of faith and also a man of great human wisdom. It is marvelous to watch him direct a discussion, resolve a conflict, reconcile a husband and wife, or the members of a family. He knows how to listen and he never interrupts. He helps them to see the other person's point of view, to envisage other solutions than those they have found themselves. His training was not such as to cut him off from the people, as happens in the case of university graduates, and the fact that he is married also links him with his human environment." (A *mokambi* studies two years full-time, or three years part-time [night school], at the Institute for Religious Studies; there is then a period of practical experience in the apostolate.)

The "priest leader" does not live in the parish; he has another full-time ministry. He could be considered a chaplain. Fr. Allary comes to St. Lawrence on Sundays and two or three nights a week.

"My duty is to perform those tasks that are properly sacerdotal: preaching and the administration of the sacraments. Besides these, my principal duty is to train others. I trained the *mokambi* when he was just starting, but now I am rather his advisor and I work with him in the training of the many lay persons who are with him."

As a matter of fact, a *mokambi*, with his "secular" profession and his family, and a "priest leader" who comes by three times a week are not enough to meet the needs of a large parish, even when the base communities themselves assume a certain number of tasks. To help, there is first of all the wife of the *mokambi* who, in addition to being the mother of a large family, looks after the women (sewing courses, etc.), and directs the women's groups of the Legion of Mary (about four hundred strong and the pillar of the parish according to the *mokambi*). Then there are all those who take charge of preparing others for the sacraments, the catechumenate for adults, youth groups, the liturgy—the Mass of Zaire—and the like.

At the same time, the parishes confined to the *bakambi* are those recently established in the new extensions of the city. They are made up of manual laborers, minor officials, and persons out of work. They are the ones who were hardest hit by the famous "evil of Zaire," which was a combination of corruption, injustice, and inefficiency. When I was in Kinshasa in 1978, most families could afford only one meal a day. Everywhere I heard the same thing: "There is too much suffering."

"We don't have the resources to help these people. From time to time something comes through from Caritas or from a collection taken up among the base communities. We get ten or twenty zaires, the parish adds what it can and we buy a sack of rice to give to those most in need" [1 zaire = approx. 17 cents USA, October 1982].

There is as well in the parish a "development committee," which organized a work party to put the roads back in shape, drew up a dossier in order to bring electricity into the zone, collected two hundred zaires—out of two thousand needed—for the construction of a bridge across the river. . . . Some persons wanted to start a hennery for the community but there were no funds. Given the needs of the moment, there is still an enormous amount to do.

"We learned bad habits during the time of the missionaries," explains the *mokambi* of St. Lawrence. The people waited for everything to come to them from the missionaries; the Christians sat back and crossed their arms. Now that the parish is run by lay persons, they are beginning to understand that it is *our* business."

This is one of the fruits to come from the appointment of *bakambi*. The experiment is too new to allow for definitive conclusions. "It is difficult to know where we are going to go with this," said Fr. Allary, "to know whether we are still on the way to something different or whether we will continue with what we have."

Cardinal Malula expressed it this way: "The confiding of parishes to lay persons is a sign of the times. Where is it going to take us? I do not wish to prophesy, but the Spirit may allow us to discover new ways of doing things that he would like to see come about."

•

Mindouli: a station on the Congo-Ocean railroad line that links Brazzaville with Pointe-Noire. It is also the center of a parish whose diamond-shaped territory measures ninety-three miles across at its widest point and forty-three miles at its narrowest point. It contains only forty-five thousand inhabitants, six large Catholic communities (*dibundu*, the plural of *mabundu*), and twenty-five small communities.

It is snowing. At least that is what the local residents call this light drizzle; they have never seen the large white flakes that fall in our northern latitudes. A message is left at the crossroads in case Maurice arrives by another road as we go to look for him on the road to Kingoyi. Soon we see him: he is coming slowly because he has injured his foot. Having started at four in the morning, he has covered some six miles, limping all the way.

We make a half-turn and set out on the road to Ntadi; it is deeply rutted. On board the heaving Land Rover we make room

for Fr. Jubault, a French priest (Fidei Donum), Joseph, retired
from public office, now president of the parish council of Mindouli, Maurice, former school principal, now vice-president
of the parish council, and André, tailor and catechist.

Every year, for four months, the members of the central parish council go to visit the *mabundu*. Today the visit is to a particularly difficult area. "We have been working here for ten years
and have hardly succeeded in building solid communities. The
residents are baptized but they remain impregnated with paganism: many practice polygamy, and the magicians still play an
important role in the life of the villages."

Ntadi: a few huts and, off to the side, the large damaged wing
of a building resting on shaky walls. This is what remains of a
chapel destroyed by a tornado. The community had just bought
it—it had been a courthouse—and its ruin had discouraged the
Catholics who live in the surrounding villages. It is to the raising
up of both the one and the other, the chapel and the community,
that Joseph, Maurice, and André are going to dedicate their
efforts, while Fr. Jubault continues on his way. The first thing to
do is reconstitute the governing body of the *dibundu*, and then
to animate it to start once again the meetings for prayer every
Sunday, and to organize a *zola* ("work group"), to rebuild the
chapel.

After the liturgy of the word the discussion can begin. The
elders of the community begin by speaking of the difficulties
they have encountered these past few weeks. Then each person
talks about his grievances and desires. The discussion ends with
the reorganization of the *dibundu*. Joseph and his companions
address the group: "From now on, you will have to get to work.
You need to meet each Sunday and take part in the *zola* for the
chapel."

In principle, every member of a *dibundu* is supposed to give a
half-day of work every week to the community. This is the case
at Kingoyi, where Maurice lives. We will see there some thirty
women busy pulling up the grass around the church in order to
prevent a brush fire that could destroy the fruit trees planted by
the *dibundu*. Sometimes a community will hire out its services to
someone who has need in order to till a field or harvest the man-

ioc. The money thus earned goes to provide meals for the priest and members of the parish council when they come to visit, or to replace a part of the chapel roof, to buy a tom-tom or some sheet music, or something else.

•

An oil lamp is set up on an old barrel in back of the church. Around it are gathered the members of the Catholic community of Mbanza-Ndounga, a large village about thirty miles from Brazzaville. There is just a hint of coolness after a scorching day, and the mosquitoes and other insects are biting. Just a few minutes before, as the sun set, children attacked a termite hill to catch—and eat—the winged ants.

Here as elsewhere the local choir is the heart of the community. The choirs were founded first of all to sing and pray at wakes for the dead among Christians—and for non-Christians, if they wished. They were also involved in all the major events of family life: the presentation of a newly born baby and its mother, a marriage, the end of a mourning period, and important anniversaries. Little by little, the choirs became the focal point for the most active of the faithful.

At Mbanza-Ndounga the choir organizes the *zola* every Wednesday. In addition to maintaining the church and feeding guests, the money earned by the community work goes to helping the sick. "We have at present six persons for whom we buy rice and dried fish." They also cultivate a garden for an old woman.

One of the choir members said to me: "When you belong to the choir, you are never again poor or sad. When there is some problem, the choir group comes to help. It is as though we made up one and the same family."

The lamp burns on. A passage from St. Paul is read and the leader of the choir comments on it. Other choir members then express their own views in Lari, the language of the tribe that makes up this part of the Congo Republic. Next, the skins on the tom-toms are heated up near the fire, and the *gongis*, metal cones that are rung by being tapped with a rod, are brought out.

Soon, under the direction of Martine, a very thin woman with incredible energy, the music and the chant begin together. Human warmth, joy, and fellowship reign in the small group, all but lost in the immense night of Africa.

Chapter 7

'

SOUTH KOREA: "DON'T COME TO MIDNIGHT MASS!"

It is Sunday morning in the countryside of South Korea. A burst of bows and smiles greets us along the dusty road where the bus has just set us down. We return the bows, awkwardly no doubt. The whole community of Kon-Dai has come out to meet us. The women are wearing their traditional dress: a long skirt that flows from just below the shoulders, and a petite jacket. It is time to go to church.

Everyone takes off his or her shoes before entering. There are no seats; worshipers kneel or sit on the floor, the women on the left and the men on the right. The small children are up front, then the older children, and finally the adults. We are in all about fifty persons. The service opens with a song, followed by the penitential rite, two readings, and the gospel. Kim Lawrence gives the homily.

Kim Lawrence is a married man, the father of five children ranging in age from nine to twenty-two. He is a farmer who lives by his crops: rice, barley, pimento, berries. Ever since this area was first evangelized, some seventy or eighty years earlier, the missions or annexes to the parish have been under the care of laymen. Since Vatican II the training these men receive has been more solid, and they have been given more responsibility, in keeping with their deepened competence. Kim Lawrence attended three sessions of three or four days each at the archbishop's residence in Andong. There were courses in Holy Scripture, theology, pedagogy, and the like. "Those sessions have been a great help in preparing liturgies at which there would be no priest. In the old days, we used to recite litanies and read something, but it had no relationship to the Mass. Now, our liturgy of the word is the same as at the eucharistic celebrations." Every week, a sermon outline and commentaries are provided for the leaders of the one hundred fifty missions attached to the twenty parishes of the diocese. "The priest who draws up these texts uses technical words and his ideas have to be translated into a language the faithful can understand. We usually give some real-life examples in order to make the gospel come alive."

After the homily, there is a creed, and then a prayer said in union with all those who are celebrating the eucharist elsewhere. Perhaps a day will come when a delegate will be sent to the parish church and the eucharist distributed during the mission services. "We've talked about it, but we are waiting for the people themselves to express such a desire." The man who told me this was Fr. Roger Doc, a priest of the Foreign Missions of Paris, and pastor of Ta-In, the parish to which Kon-Dai, along with fifteen other communities, is attached.

●

Kim Lawrence, our host, receives us in a room of his hemp-mat house. A television set presides in one corner. The floor is warm: a network of pipes carries the heat from the kitchen fire to the rest of the house. This is *ondol*: central heating Korean-style.

A sizable portion of the Catholic community is gathered in the yard of the house. There are eighty-three Catholics on the registers of the mission, out of the total hamlet population of eight hundred. There are Protestants here as well—relations between the two groups are very poor (Fr. Doc tells the Catholics they are not to punch back)—and there are Buddhists. Everybody is named either Kim or Choi. "The Chois are lukewarm whether they be Catholic or Protestant." The names of the three are Kim Agatha, Kim Anna, and Kim Suzanne. The conversation is decidedly limited because of our total ignorance of the Korean language. Fortunately, Fr. Doc arrives on his motorbike. The meal consists of a mixture of rice and barley served wth *kimchi,* a traditional dish, which is a sort of sauerkraut made from fermented cabbage or turnips seasoned with pimentos.

Fr. Doc was happy over a rather surprising victory. He had succeeded in persuading the leaders of the parish missions not to come to the parish church at Ta-In for the midnight Mass at Christmas and Easter, as they had been accustomed to doing. "I asked them to stay in their local communities so that they could celebrate the feast days with those who could not come to the central parish church: the elderly, mothers, and small children. The evening can be organized with songs, dances, plays, and so forth."

In the diocese of Andong there are twenty-seven thousand Catholics, in a total population of about 1.7 million. Over half the Catholics live in villages where there is no priest. In the parish centers laymen have also been placed in positions of responsibility, but there are more difficulties in such a situation. The ones chosen are businessmen, government officials, or teachers, and they have less time than their rural counterparts to devote to meetings or training sessions. In addition, as bishop Dumont of Andong told me, there have been cases where the lay leader began to consider himself the overall leader of the community and relegated the priest to an exclusively sacramental ministry. This had to be counteracted.

•

We accompany Fr. Doc, walking along a dirt road. During the week this is the way he visits the missions, whether on foot, by bus, or by bicycle. The satellite community farthest from Ta-In is nine miles away. "The communities out on the missions are more alive than at the center." This remark by Fr. Doc I heard repeated in Africa and Latin America, as well as in Asia. "I was able to spend six months in France; the Christian community life continued on here."

We are heading for a village that, from a distance, looks like any other. Here a man is fixing a tool outside his house; there a woman is molding bricks. There are about one hundred persons living here, of whom a good number are children. They make their living by farming. Most of them are Catholics. They make up one of the missions of the parish, and it is a "good" mission: they all live grouped around the chapel and this facilitates community life. They are lepers.

We sit down in the sacristy with the leader of the community. He is an elderly man whose face is marked by his disease. He hands over the collection to Fr. Doc. The lepers contribute like everyone else to the material support of the central parish. Each of the faithful donates one day's income a month. It is out of this that they are able to give something to the priest, cover the expenses of a teaching session, and share in the expenses of the diocese. "It is also a way to express our faith."

Chapter 8

LATIN AMERICA:
MINISTERS OF THE WORD

Chile

We are in Santiago, in a *población*—a poor section of the city made up of wooden huts that look for all the world like the sheds you generally find in a backyard. There is a little chapel. One priest, a non-Chilean, has the care of three parishes whose total population is about fifty thousand. He is helped by two Canadian lay missionaries. This means that the bulk of the pastoral work must be carried out by the lay persons of the *población*: shop workers, manual workers, and not a few who are out of work.

We go to a meeting of the "ministers of the word." There are six men there, chosen from among the elders of the community. "Those men are preferred whose family life is in order, all the more because the wife shares in the duties of her husband." They were appointed by the episcopal vicar for the area; the local priest laid hands on them at the feast of Pentecost.

"We meet every Friday to prepare the Sunday liturgy, be it the Mass or a celebration without a priest. Usually we give the homily; we try to apply the biblical texts to the realities of our everyday life."

There are ministers for the other sacraments as well. Three couples are responsible for preparing (in four meetings) and

49

administering baptism. For first communion, both parents and children must attend a meeting once a week for two years under the direction of "guides" who have themselves received the same training. "It is really a matter of catechism for adults. We try to 'convert' them and urge them to join the community. In this way we try to make sure that the children will receive support from their families and don't give up the practice of their faith after their first communion."

Marriages—and there are four a month—are also prepared and celebrated by lay ministers: "qualified witnesses" of the sacrament. A team of three couples gathers the prospective marriage partners together and, over the course of six evenings, speaks with them about sexual relations, the Christian meaning of marriage, a budget, relations between parents and children, and the like. The priest is called in only when there are canonical problems.

Lay persons are also responsible for youth activities, the aged, visiting the sick, conducting funerals, preparing candidates for confirmation, and similar functions.

•

Another parish in Santiago. Two priests for one hundred thousand persons living in *poblaciones*—the poorest of the poor. There is no church building ("and there won't be one for as long as possible"); members gather by district. "In fact this parish is a federation of communities." One of the communities is led by a married deacon, the father of eight children. He welcomes me into his home—a hut that has been fixed up—into his tiny office where a tabernacle dominates.

"I lead the liturgy of the word on the Sundays when there is no Mass. I teach catechism, celebrate baptisms and marriages, receive those who want to talk to me about their problems, visit those who no longer come to our meetings. . . ." He is given no remuneration for his services and his employment as a photographer earns him a pitifully small income. "He helps me," he said, pointing to the tabernacle. "I used to keep records and they never balanced. Now I don't keep any records; I just rely on the Lord."

Bishop Hourton, the auxiliary responsible for the southern

part of Santiago, told me: "We are making every effort to foster the base communites and decentralize the parishes." For his part a theologian said: "This is easier to do in a city where the *población* constitutes a living reality and where the people have a keen sense of neighborliness than it would be in a large impersonal city of individualistic Europe."

This pastoral approach is being adopted by the country parishes as well, such as that of Futrono in the south of Chile. This parish territory is seventy-five miles in length and has sixteen or seventeen thousand inhabitants. "We have at present twenty-three communities," said the pastor, a Frenchman, Fr. Jacques Fournier. "Some of them have been in existence about ten years; others are very recent. They support one another. It is through them that the church exercises an influence."

At Futrono the leaders are chosen by the people. They come three or four times a year to the center, often walking many hours to get there, to attend training sessions. There are discussions concerning the material needs of the communities as well as those concerning the faith or the liturgy. In addition to these sessions, Fr. Fournier visits them regularly and sends them literature.

All of these communities and groups directed by lay persons presuppose an enormous effort at Christian education. There is a center in Santiago that has published one million four hundred thousand copies of various books and brochures in the last five years—in addition to organizing courses in adult religious education.

When I spoke to the director of the center, he told me: "Every one of these courses for adults comprises at least fifty hours of lectures and discussions. Last year, we had two thousand six hundred 'students' who came from Santiago and other parts of the country. In January, during vacation season, we had twelve hundred lay persons in this house. All of them, except for four, came from poor areas."

One night I went to one of the sessions and I asked some of the persons there why they had come. Here are two of their answers.

"What I learn here makes me happy, and I want to share it with those who live in my part of the city."

"I got up at six o'clock to go to work, and after work I was tired, but I came all the same because I am responsible for many others. God will never fail us; I don't want to fail him either." Then she added as everyone laughed ("we love to laugh; it's the only thing that doesn't cost too much these days"): "We need doctrine like an alcoholic needs wine."

Nicaragua

Everything around us is dark green. We are surrounded by fruit trees: banana, orange, coconut, mango, acacia. . . . In the sky, sqadrons of *chocoyos*—I am told they always fly in pairs— are going through their maneuvers. The sulphuric vapors from the volcano named Santiago have once again spared this village of the same name and have not dried up the trees and corroded the tin roofs on the houses.

We are in Nicaragua, a few months after the victory of the Sandinista revolution, among *campesinos* ("peasants") who for the most part own minuscule plots of land on which, with a machete, they cultivate corn and kidney beans. To make a little money they go to work on the large coffee plantations such as that formerly owned by the Somoza family. It was nationalized by the new regime. They also try to make money by getting themselves hired as day laborers in Managua, the capital.

It is the end of the day. A table and benches have been brought and set up in the yard of a small house made of wood and brick. The women and children are seated. The men are standing in back of them and on the other side of the dirt road along the hedge of cactus, a little bit apart. There are certainly more than two hundred persons gathered here.

We begin by singing—not exactly *together*, but that is not important. Then Gerardo Guevara, minister of the word, reads the passage in St. Luke on the "useless servants" (Luke 17:10). He gives a commentary on the text and the other ministers of the word give their reflections in turn. They speak of the humility of Christ, and they also speak of the revolution.

"Warfare is not the only kind of revolution. You know what war is, with the dead and wounded and destruction everywhere! The revolution that Christ wants is a revolution of peace and love, a revolution of humility and patience. . . ."

We are inundated by a sudden shower. Everyone seeks refuge in the house or under the trees. When the rain stops the celebration recommences. We pray for each other's intentions. Right beside us a woman is grinding coffee beans with a stone and the sound she makes is in rhythm with our prayer. There is then another song and we end with the Our Father.

For four years now the community at Santiago has met like this each day. There are not always as many as today—our visit attracted a good number—but I was told that there are usually from fifty to a hundred persons from a village of seventy houses.

•

The parish center is in the market town of San Marcos. It is here that the ministers of the word for the seven parishes of the department of Carazo are trained. All this began five or six years earlier as a result of the initiative of a Canadian priest, Fr. Benito Laplante. There are now more than three hundred men and women involved, from among the poor for the most part. They begin by taking an introductory course lasting three days. Then after six months of working in their community, there is a second course of five days, and finally, at the end of a year, another course lasting five days.

On this night twenty-three of these ministers of the word are preparing themselves to participate in a week-long seminar on the theme "Christian faith and the revolution in Nicaragua." Some have come a long way: one delegate walked eleven miles before getting the bus that brought him the rest of the way. "It was through contact with the people that I understood the meaning of the beatitude of the poor in spirit," said Fr. Rosario, Fr. Benito's co-worker.

We have a meal with the delegates: rice, beans, and a small piece of cheese. I asked one of them to define for me his role. "It is to assemble the community, proclaim the word of God, and conscientize the Christians."

During that week of updating there will be discussion of what was treated during the meeting of the Latin American bishops at Puebla. They will also discuss the social teaching of the church, socialism, the bourgeois world faced with that of the proletariat—all subjects of burning interest in the Nicaraguan context.

It is thanks to these delegates that the church can be present in a remote village like Santiago or on the former plantation of the Somoza family near San Marcos, seized by the revolution and taken over by the state. One morning at six o'clock, before work begins, Fr. Benito celebrates Mass in the open air in full view of the ruins of the family house once owned by the ex-dictator. Two or three hundred *campesinos,* their machetes hanging from their arms, stand around the altar. It has been set up in the field where new housing units are being built for the workers who will come for the coffee harvest.

"Now they treat us better," said Alfonso, minister of the word and member of the union committee elected by the workers of the plantation. "They treat us like free persons and no longer like animals."

In his homily Fr. Benito spoke about agrarian reform and the national literacy campaign. He said, "The church must take its part in the revolution. We must combat illiteracy with the resources of our faith." The presence or absence of dedicated and well-trained Christians will determine what Nicaragua looks like tomorrow.

Part Three

On the Side of the Rich or the Poor?

Gustavo Gutiérrez has written: "In a society where the social classes are in conflict with one another, we are faithful to God if we take our place on the side of the poor, the working classes, the despised races, the marginated cultures. It is from this stance that we can live and proclaim the good news of the gospel" (from a study prepared for the World Missionary Conference, Melbourne, May 1980).

Makalle, the capital of the Tigre region in Ethiopia: they are selling empty tin cans to be used as dishes or bowls. Kinshasa: the heads of dried fish are being sold for 25 makutas [approx. 7 cents] each; a teacher earns the equivalent of about $29 a month. The bush land of Mozambique: a Swiss doctor spends his day in a clinic; he sees 160 patients and pulls twenty teeth; patients came on foot from as far away as thirty miles. Zimbabwe: a man has his money taken by some young thieves; they shout out at him, "Why do you bring children into the world if you cannot take care of them?" The Sudan: some women show me their heads; their hair has been completely worn off by the leather water bottles that they carry on their heads; the pump in their village broke down and they have to walk several miles every day to get water. The Peruvian Andes: a man walks with fifty pounds of potatoes on his shoulders; he is bringing them to market, a walk of many hours from his house. A restaurant in Managua, Nicaragua: a young boy wants to sell me some revolutionary decals; I turn him down; he then asks me if he can finish the rice on my plate; he devours it.

No, the human race is not exactly what we may have once thought it was. It is not made up of well dressed, well fed persons who live in a house or an apartment with hot water, television, and electrical appliances, and who are tied into a national system of social security. In our part of the world there is not much talk of famine, war, flood, or other life-threatening catastrophes. Our attention centers on the ordinary lot of persons like ourselves.

Christians have always dedicated themselves to the relief of suffering, and their work of assistance has often been indispensable. Today, more and more persons, in many different ways, are espousing the cause of the poor. Let us listen once again to Gustavo Gutiérrez:

"The gospel tells us that when the good news is preached to the poor, the kingdom is near. The poor are the ones who hope and believe in Christ; to use the term in its strict sense, they are the Christians. Is it possible to reverse this statement and say that the Christians today are the poor? Perhaps we should go even further and say that the gospel will never really be liberating until the poor themselves are its preachers" (ibid.).

Chapter 9

BOMBAY:
TWO WORLDS IN ONE

Andheri, an area near the airport. A fierce sunlight strikes against the mineral countryside: bare, gray mountains of basalt surrounding steel-blue lakes. You can just make out human figures moving against a background of dusty air. They are laborers, men and women, digging in the open quarry, breaking stones and carrying them in baskets on their heads. There are also two large red trucks and an old squeaking steam shovel.

We come closer. Just to walk in that furnace is an effort. A man about forty years old pries large blocks of stone with a steel bar. Sweat is running down his dark face. He comes from the south of India and has five children. "I make 110 rupees a month" [1 rupee = approx. 7.25 cents USA, October 1982]. A group gathers around: "Men make ten rupees a day, women seven, but there is not work every day. What we make is not enough to live on."

The workers in the quarry live right next to it in a shantytown constructed of tin sheets, wooden planks, and rags. The women do their wash in one of the lakes of the quarry. Children run about everywhere. The owners of the quarry, a rich family, refuse to build a school. This was told to me by an Indian nun. When I asked her why they refused, she simply said: "The rich want to get richer."

She belongs to a congregation known as the Helpers of Mary,

founded in Bombay by a German woman, Anna Huberta. Officially recognized by the church in 1962, the Helpers of Mary number about two hundred, all Indian. They have offered themselves to serve the very poorest and to live a life of poverty themselves. Their house is separated from the shantytown by only a wall. They have established close relationships with the five hundred families living there, with an average of six children per family.

•

The road forms a sort of dike in the middle of a black sewage ditch that gives off a fetid stench. We go down between the junkyards of scrap metal and finally come out on a cluttered road. From that point on, there is nothing but a network of alleys and paths edged with shacks, extending about as far as one can see. This is Dharavi, one of the worst slums in Asia. I was told that 160,000 persons live here.

There are eight Helpers of Mary at Dharavi. They share their very simple dwelling with fifty orphans. They have—the ultimate luxury—their own water faucet; it dispenses the precious liquid every night between seven and eight o'clock. The shantytowners in general must have recourse to a public fountain that is turned on for two hours a day. "We lived that way for ten years," said Sr. Imelda. Not an easy thing when you are running a maternity clinic.

Most of those who live in Dharavi come from rural areas and have had no employment training whatsoever. They work in the nearby tanneries, in factories, as day laborers, or they have no work at all. "We know families whose income is less than a hundred rupees a month. There is hunger here: often they have only one meal a day and it is not a good meal." The sisters give out bread, donated by the Rotary Club, to those most in need.

They also run a kindergarten to prepare children for school: three hundred children in a shack measuring thirty by sixteen feet. "If we don't take them, there is a strong possibility that they will not get any schooling." Two of the sisters lived for two years in a house in the middle of the slum. They laughingly told me, "The rain used to come in on our blankets." They finally

had to leave that place because of the continual interruptions
from their neighbors, which made it impossible to find time to
pray.

Two Helpers of Mary take me to visit some of the families. We
leave the road and enter a narrow alleyway, and finally come to a
comparatively large building. Its walls are made of planks and
tin sheets with a roof half of bamboo and half of transparent
plastic, which seals out the air. But "it doesn't really keep the
rain out."

On the earthen floor there is a pot of vegetables. Ten persons
live here. The grandfather lies stretched out on a mat; he is near
death. Then there is a man, his wife, and seven children. One of
the children has just come back from the hospital and is lying on
the one bed in the house. He is gravely ill and alarmingly thin
and pale. They all look at me with large eyes; those hungry eyes
still haunt me.

The father, who is forty-six years old, has always lived here.
He makes between 150 and 165 rupees a month (but only half of
it reaches the home). For breakfast there is a cup of tea or coffee, a piece of bread (given out by the sisters), and some vegetables from the pot on the floor. It is not surprising that everyone
here suffers from malnutrition.

Surrounded by a cloud of little boys, we walk along narrow
and dark paths full of various odors. We have to watch that we
do not bump our heads on the projecting planks that hold up the
tin roofs that nearly touch one another. We come upon a distill-
ery: "It's illegal, but it is a way of making a little money. Unfortunately, people get drunk and it leads to arguments and fights."

We walk around the chickens, goats, and pigs that freely roam
the alleyways. We pass by a nauseating pond. You could call this
place a monster village—or better yet, a thousand villages
squeezed into the space for one, pressed together by some mind-
less machine. You can tell the poor: they are the "dis-lodged."

You have to bend over double to get into the shack. There is a
woman there with her children. She has given birth to nine, but
six of them died from malnutrition or diarrhea. Her husband is
one of those who deliver merchandise by handcart. You see them
running on the city streets in among the double-decker buses and
the honking taxis, amid the hubbub, the dust, and the exhaust

fumes. Barefoot or wearing sandals, they strain against their load—sacks of vegetables, sugar cane, piles of clothes, cases of bottles, bundles of paper—pushing with all the strength of their neck and shoulders to get over a slight incline in the road. Or they try to hold their wagon back as they go down a hill, their legs stretched and their back contracted. They are soaked in sweat and their ragged robes swirl around their lean bodies.

"Usually he makes seven or eight rupees a day," his wife told me. "Yesterday he worked from nine in the morning until six at night for nine rupees—and I just spent seven rupees for a box of paper tissues. The problem is that he cannot find merchandise to transport every day. The monsoon season in particular is a slack period for the men who push handcarts. During that period we have to borrow in order to have money to buy rice, and we pay back when there is work once again."

They already had to borrow once when they still lived in the Madras region. Victimized by a loan shark, they were forced to sell their tiny plot of land and come to Bombay to look for a way to subsist.

•

A high wall made of stone. On the other side, the runways of the airport of Bombay on which move the jumbo jets, the DC 10s, and the other aircraft. You hear the roar of the jet motors and smell their fumes. I know the inside of those planes very well: the plush surroundings, the businessmen, the tourists, the newspaper and television journalists. Comfortably installed in their seats, they open up the *Times of India* given to them by a stewardess.

On this side of the wall, huts jammed between it and the sewer ditch, all but smothered by tree leaves. The huts have a very somber appearance, with their walls of woven bamboo soiled by mud and their roofs of tin or scraps of canvas. This minislum houses some two hundred persons. "They have come in from the countryside because they owned no land there and they had no way to get food in the village."

About thirty children are crowded into an enclosure made of branches. A blackboard leans up against a hut. This is the school

run by the Missionary Brothers of Charity (the masculine counterpart of the sisterhood founded by Mother Teresa). They try to
teach these children how to read. They cannot attend an ordinary school, because they have to work: they salvage paper,
wood, metal, and they beg at the airport.

The brothers give out food, visit the families, and care for the
people. "We teach them not to wash in the sewer ditch, because
they get skin diseases that way." There are four brothers, all
Indians, living in a ramshackle house (no running water) in a
poor sector of the city. Two of them work in this slum and the
other two work especially with lepers.

We stop by a bed, just beside a small hut. There is a woman
lying there; her thick black hair is streaked with gray. She is
about forty years old. There is a cup of water in her hand. A few
drops have trickled down her dark cheek and run onto her emaciated chest (you could count her ribs). She is suffering from
diarrhea but obstinately refuses to go to the hospital because she
does not want to leave her two little daughters (she has no husband). "If I have to die, I'd rather die here," she keeps repeat-
ing.

I wanted somebody to do something at any cost to save her,
but the brothers admitted their powerlessness. "These people
accept their lot." It is but one woman among so many others
who are going to die. A few days from now, I will be on the
other side of this wall in one of those airplanes whose motors are
ringing in our ears. How is it possible that we can live in two
worlds that are so different?

●

Yesterday Mother Teresa opened a new "dying room" in Bombay. She spoke a few words to us and it sounded like a page out
of the gospel.

"Even after all these years I have never seen anyone die among
us who had hate, bitterness, or despair in their heart. No one has
ever refused the love offered them. Three nights ago, we found a
woman in very bad condition. I did what I could for her and at
the end there was a splendid smile on her face. She thanked me
and died. She never complained at having been left out in the

street with no food and no one to care for her; she didn't complain about dying. She only said 'thank you.' That is how our people are!"

There was no atmosphere of drama or horror to be found in the "dying room," but rather a great peace, an aura of serenity. An Indian sociologist said to me: "You must not look at the misery with Western eyes. The people in the slums have an astounding capacity to survive and their human worth does not depend on the conditions in which they live." It is true: the women's saris somehow remain immaculate amid all the squalor. It is true: you find an incredible gentleness, smiles, and laughter among the poor.

"More than a thousand persons assembled Tuesday morning at ten o'clock in front of the municipal building of Janata Colony and broke through the thin line of policemen protecting the building. The demonstrators dumped garbage in front of the offices in protest against the negligence of the authorities in not removing the garbage dumps at Cheetah Camp." This story appeared a short time ago in the *Times of India*.

That same day the municipality cleaned up the Cheetah Camp, a slum. This is an example of the activity of BUILD (Bombay Urban Industrial League for Development). It is an ecumenical group with sixteen full-time and thirty-six part-time workers.

I spoke with Rajan Singh, the secretary general. "After this, we, along with the people at Cheetah Camp, reflected on these events. We asked ourselves why the slums are neglected like that when the people who live in them are making a real contribution to the wealth of the country."

BUILD also runs a health program as well as education for children and adults. "We offer services, we give people training, and we help them organize themselves for action."

At Jaffer Baba Colony, 167 families (about fifteen hundred persons) went eighteen years without any drinking water even though funds had been allotted to bring electricity there and construct public toilets that flush with water. Nothing happened and the money disappeared. "It took nine months of work and protest to arrive at a solution."

Implementation of the project meant that some of the huts

had to be displaced. Slumdwellers decided to profit by this and build more stable dwellings. At a meeting they decided to parcel out the land in equal plots (until then the plots had been of unequal sizes), to call in but one or two experts, and have the rest of the work done by the families who would live there.

A hard-fought battle had to be waged with the city administration; it considered the proposed dimensions of individual plots to be excessive: twenty square yards was "too much" for a working-class family. Finally, a low-interest loan was secured.

"We didn't want to use foreign money for this project, because the people would have found some pretext later on for not paying it back. That's how you make beggars out of them," Rajan Singh said to me.

The small houses are being built now—eighty-six are finished—but the residents of Jaffer Baba Colony still are not secure yet. The land does not belong to them; it is officially considered vacant. This means that any plan for urbanizing the area could be put into effect with no account taken of the existence of Jaffer Baba Colony.

That is why there was formed the "United Front of the Slumdwellers of Bombay," which already represents 200,000 persons in fifty-five slum areas. Its chief goal is precisely to have a piece of land allotted to each family. As Rajan Singh said: "The Son of Man had nowhere to lay his head. That is the life of the poor in Bombay."

Bombay is considered to be the richest city in India, and thus it has a strong attraction for those who live in rural areas. This invasion creates an enormous housing problem. Slightly less than half of its seven million inhabitants live in one of the eight hundred slum areas of the city, and some two hundred thousand others have opted to live on its sidewalks. Another segment of the population has found refuge in the single-room apartments that are often no better than a slum. I saw a building whose facade had collapsed. However, this did not prevent many families from still living there, as in some human-sized doll house.

I asked the archbishop of Bombay, Bishop Simon Pimenta, if Catholics show any awareness of the misery that pervades their city.

"I'm afraid not. We have mostly Catholics of the traditional type who are satisfied with coming to Mass on Sunday. They have their job and their house, and they are satisfied with their life. They don't see any need for getting involved in the struggle against poverty. There are some priests, some women religious, and some seminarians who are active in this field, and I think that it is thanks to them that a social awareness is growing, especially among the young."

Catholics are a minority in India, well known for their schools and hospitals. "These institutions were able to answer adequately to the needs of the past but today they make up but a small part of what is needed. I would say about 10 percent." This was the estimate of Fr. Sidney D'Souza, a Jesuit who directs the social center of Seva Niketan, which is also involved in working in the slum areas.

"There are many ways of working with the poor, and they do not exclude one another. Nevertheless in our day we have to put the accent on conscientization. It is a question of organizing people, helping them discover their rights, and fight so that these rights are respected. This means taking risks. The church seems to prefer the security of its petty privileges to this prophetic role. The question is whether we wish truly to witness to Christ and take him seriously, or whether we will hang on to our security before all else."

This is a question that faces the Christians of Bombay. It could be facing others as well.

Chapter 10

CHILE:
MINISTRY OF SOLIDARITY

Children in a yard, some barefoot, are dancing in a circle singing a nursery song about chocolates. They have just come out of a building made of planks and have been replaced by other children who are getting ready for the second sitting. They receive on their plate some potatoes and carrots and a piece of chicken—chicken because it is a holiday.

This is their only meal of the day. I asked one of the mothers what these children ate at home; it was a stupid blunder! She could not answer me except with a flow of tears. It is because the men out of work—and even some who work but are badly paid—cannot feed their families that *comedores* ("soup kitchens") had to be opened.

"At first the mothers experience a great humiliation in needing to have recourse to a *comedor*. Then they see that they are not the only ones with this problem, and they understand better the meaning of solidarity."

This was María, a Chilean girl about twenty years old who was accompanying me. She is in charge of four *comedores* run by the Catholic and Protestant parishes of this *población*. "The big danger," she said, "is that the people get used to handouts; but there isn't any alternative."

Nevertheless this *comedor* is not an ordinary soup kitchen. Care is taken that parents themselves operate the kitchen.

Mothers go to the market to beg for unsold fruits and vegetables, and take turns doing the cooking. Fathers cultivate a community garden. From time to time a collection is taken up in the *población* among those who still have work. "If a mother does not want to participate in the activities of the *comedor*, we have to send her child home."

María was just about to faint, so she had to leave me and go home. She has a stomach ulcer—probably the result of the night of interrogation by the police and her being dismissed from the university—and she had had a hemorrhage that morning. She was under suspicion because of "social activities" she took part in during the regime of President Allende. She left me with a sort of smile, saying, "I feel old; I have seen so much."

Together with a Canadian lay missionary, I go to visit a family. There is one room furnished with a bed, a sofa, and two worn-out chairs. There is another room for the six children and a corner for the kitchen. In back, a yard, where the wash is drying. The father of the family is repairing shoes; it is not his profession. "I am a construction worker but I have had no work for two months. Before that I was out of work for eleven months."

He has no unemployment compensation. As is the case with many in the poor sections of the city, he had to sell, at a cheap price, all the things that he owned: his watch, his wife's watch, their sewing machine, and the radio. He explained: "You can live without a watch, you can live without a sewing machine or a radio, but you can't live without food."

For the moment his only income derives from *pololos*, "odd jobs," such as working on the shoes someone had asked him to fix. "I make just enough to buy four loaves of bread a day." It would be very difficult to feed eight persons on four loaves of bread a day and some tea. What saves them is the *comedor*.

"What do your children need?" (One would be embarrassed to ask such a question of a father whose children do not need anything.)

"Shoes, warm clothes for the winter. . . we can no longer afford to buy notebooks and the schoolbooks that they need." Later on he added: "The most important thing is work. I am used to working for my living and not receiving handouts. But for the moment I have to accept the situation."

"He doesn't drink and he doesn't smoke; these are the kind of people who always lived poorly but looked after themselves," the lay missionary told me. Nevertheless many men cannot take this humiliation and sink into alcoholism, abandon their families, or even commit suicide. Nervous tension and psychosomatic illnesses are rampant in the *poblaciones*. All of this has a disturbing effect on the hundreds of thousands of young children and adolescents who, left more or less on their own, are forced to eke out a living by selling chewing gum or toothbrushes—if they do not turn to thievery and prostitution.

Faced with this situation, the people created special funds for those out of work in order to activate a flow of mutual help and moral support among the victims. These funds were used in an attempt to establish independent workshops for weaving, embroidery, woodwork, or for the raising of rabbits and chickens. But they came up against enormous difficulties, especially because of the lack of an outlet for what they produced.

In the parish where I was visiting there were workshops for sewing, shoe repair, and baking. They had tried to manufacture belts from pieces of discarded leather but they had given it up because it took too long. In addition the parish has a dispensary that enables it to take care of those who, after three months of unemployment, lost their right to unemployment benefits. There was also a center that provided notebooks and pencils to students who needed them, and awarded some scholarships for study. All of this was done with the aid of a Protestant group and the vicariate of the Catholic diocese, working together.

This vicariate, which is part of the diocese of Santiago, coordinates the "ministry of solidarity" established by the Catholic church with the collaboration of other churches in Chile and abroad to alleviate the sufferings of the Chilean people.

"We don't claim that we are resolving the problem, but this action is a sign. It shows that the church is close to the poor."

A bishop said to me, "The church has chosen the poor." That statement surely needs to be nuanced because, as is true in many other places also, the Chilean church is divided. Yet there are examples of a movement—even physical—on the part of certain ecclesiastical structures in favor of the poorer areas. Thus, some religious left their large schools to live in small communities in the *poblaciones*. Someone said: "It's getting hard to find priests for the bourgeoisie."

"Most priests maintain contact with the poor. The parish can no longer restrict itself to matters of worship without becoming aware of the problems facing the faithful. These problems have become so grave that it is impossible to ignore them."

Of course it is not that the church has only now concerned itself with the social field and brought its help to those least favored by society. What is new, according to theologian Segundo Galilea, is that the church has begun to align itself with the poor no matter what the cost. "It is not the help offered to those who live in insecurity but rather the insecurity in which the church is willing to put itself that lets the poor know that the church is *their* church and their hope."

We have to admit, however, that the presence of the church in the midst of the Chilean people is still quite a limited reality. You can find in a *población* one thousand active Christians out of seventy thousand inhabitants. Elsewhere there are about eight hundred persons at a Sunday Mass out of forty thousand who live in the district. Nevertheless this contact is transforming the church. A bishop could say to me: "The poor are evangelizing us."

Chapter 11

EGYPT: NUNS AMONG THE RAGPICKERS

From a distance you would say that it looks like a mound with a few scrawny palm trees growing on it. We go along a field of *khobeza* (a soup ingredient) and we come upon a kind of rust-colored wall: it is the backs of huts made of bent tin sheets. We pass by men who are cutting up old cans with tin snips. The metal that they obtain will be used in making electrical equipment.

We go down into the village. The first thing that hits you is the odor, a stench that nearly knocks you over. Little by little you get used to it and finally you forget it—almost. As we walked along, we began to realize that we were walking on a layer of garbage and that everything around us was garbage. We were treated to a scene of pigs crowning a hill of waste disposal while the sun set behind them. And then there were the dogs and the flies. Luckily it was not summer!

Sr. Emmanuelle and Sr. Sarah are walking ahead of me. Some readers may have heard of Sr. Emmanuelle. When over sixty years of age, she left the school in Cairo where she had been teaching, in order to come and live among the ragpickers. She wrote about this in a book (Emmanuelle Cinquin, *Chiffonnière avec les chiffonniers,* Paris: Ed. Ouvrières, 1977). Sr. Sarah, who is Egyptian, belongs to the Coptic Orthodox congregation of the Daughters of Mary, founded in 1966 by Bishop Athanasios, the bishop of Beni Suef.

This is the first time that Coptic religious have left their convent to go to work among the poor. There are five of them. They live in a modest rented dwelling in a village in the full throes of expansion next to the garbage-dump village in Azbet El Makhl. One of the religious is a nurse and runs a dispensary, another directs a workshop. The others visit the families, teach hygiene and sewing, and discuss with the women how to space the births of their children.

In the early-morning mist that surrounds us one can just make out a cart being pulled by three donkeys. This is how the garbage arrives. Earlier, at about four or five o'clock, the man and one of his sons, or a nephew, had left for a sector of Cairo about nine miles from here. Having arrived at the street that the "boss" had allotted to him, the man climbed up the stairs from floor to floor, knocking at the doors. The occupants emptied their garbage pails into his basket. Meanwhile the child—he must have been about four or five years old—stayed in the cart, numbed by the cold of winter, to watch the donkeys.

By "ragpickers" we must understand "scavengers." They provide the garbage pickup for the capital of Egypt. They then sort it out for recycling. They separate the paper, cardboard, glass, and metal to be resold. Except for the orange peels, which are strewn everywhere, the organic garbage goes to feed the pigs, and sometimes human beings: five children gulped down the contents of a can of meat that had gone rancid; two of them are dead now.

As we walk along, Sisters Emmanuelle and Sarah are surrounded by the children, and there are hugs and shouts dominated by the piercing voice of Sr. Emmanuelle. The adults come up to them as well, without any timidity. The miracle, at least to my European eyes, is that there is happiness on the faces of these children smeared with filth, that there is light in the eyes of these men who shake our hand, and that there is a smile on the lips of the women. In such a place! "Oh yes, we live in joy!" exclaims Sr. Emmanuelle.

We go to where Sr. Emmanuelle lives, a shack formerly used for goats, in the middle of the slum. We open the padlock, push on the door, and find ourselves in a room measuring about eight by six feet, furnished with a bed. Cracks in the boards let the daylight in; "You see, we even have air conditioning!"

"When I am here I am the most fortunate woman in the world. It is said that Christ is our spouse, and these are not just words. In this place we are aware of him almost visibly and tangibly. It is a daily life of intimacy with him. It is marvelous. Human life is a mystery. The more we try to have, the poorer we become spiritually. The more we divest ourselves and share, the richer we become."

•

Together with Sr. Sarah we go to visit a family. We pass through a yard full of chickens and then enter a room. Though the walls are made of tin, the room is much cleaner than one would have imagined. "The women take care of the interior of their houses." Two brothers and their wives are in front of me; they are leaning against a large bed covered with a counterpane embroided with letters of the Arabic alphabet.

"We come from a village in upper Egypt near Asyut. There was not enough land there for everyone."

We are offered a cup of tea and I ask what they eat here in this village. "Bread, cheese, *foul* (an Egyptian dish consisting mainly of beans), lentils, and vegetables."

No one will die of hunger in Egypt at least so long as the government maintains the very low price of *baladi* (a sort of pita bread). Even fish and meat are within reach if they are bought at a cooperative. But this does not mean that the ragpickers are satisfied with their lot.

"There is nothing good here, but I have to stay in order to make a living."

"How could you better your situation?"

"If the 'boss' let us have a little more money, things would go better, but he keeps it all for himself."

The "boss" is the person who, along with some assistants, has control over the garbage pickup in Cairo. You have to go to him if you wish to get involved in this work. It is he, it seems, who provides the cart and the donkeys, and assigns the ragpickers their various sectors of the city. All have to give to him most of the money that the citizens of Cairo pay in order to have their garbage picked up. Nobody knows where he gets his power, and the answers to the questions that I asked here and there did not shed much light on the mystery that surrounds him. One of the ragpickers told me that he is "crazy with money"—that is, very rich.

As Sr. Sarah said: "Our people carry out a task that is useful for the community. It isn't that they want to stop doing this, but the living conditions must be changed. Particularly, we have to separate the garbage and the pigs from the human beings."

It seems that in government circles there is some thought of establishing the ragpickers on sites where they could build real houses. At the moment they do not have the right to do this—on land they rent from rural landowners. Then the garbage would be taken farther away. Nothing would be gained by replacing the ragpickers by garbagemen with their trucks and a huge incinerator. The most important factor is the future of the people.

When she first came to the garbage-dump village, Sr. Emmanuelle began by starting a kindergarten in a hut that faces her cabin. The idea was to prepare the young ragpickers for entrance into the government school. Success was only partial: a hundred out of a thousand were accepted into the school. One of them is named Fares. He is oldest of the four sons and two daughters of one of the two couples whom we are visiting (the other couple has no children).

"There are forty-eight pupils in my class, but I am the only one from the garbage dump. The others don't like me; I have no friends. They say that I come from the ragpickers' place, that I have a bad odor."

In European society the children of the Fourth World often experience the same prejudice; they suffer the same kind of exclusion. Without a doubt the most precious thing that Sr. Emmanuelle brought to the ragpickers by going to live among them was the recognition of their dignity. "We never stop talking to them about their dignity," Sr. Sarah told me. "It is the meaning of our presence here."

Someone takes us to the nearby chapel of the garbage-dump village. At present, it is made of tin, as are all the houses, but the ragpickers have pledged themselves to build a church. A rug is on the ground; there are pictures of the Virgin and the Last Supper. Sr. Sarah whispers to me: "God is here in the midst of the poor."

Though there are also Moslems, there are a good number of Christians—Coptic Orthodox—among the ragpickers. Every two weeks on Monday morning a priest comes to celebrate Mass. Every evening about fifty persons meet for prayer under the direction of a deacon.

The mother of Fares told me: "We know that God loves us because he sends us priests, deacons, and sisters."

•

Just as we are leaving the village the uproar of a violent argument reaches our ears. Instantly, Sr. Emmanuelle and Sr. Sarah hurry toward the hut that is the source of the noise. The men calm down little by little, but there are dramatic interludes.

"Where can they go at night? There is nothing else for them to do but go to the café where they drink adulterated alcohol for six piasters [= approx. 12 cents USA, October 1982] per liter. They get drunk, they fight, and finish by drawing their knives."

A short distance from the village there is a complex built for the ragpickers, Salam Center. Others who live nearby and who are also quite poor are not excluded. There is already a dispensary, a kindergarten that replaces the shack that Sr. Emmanuelle used, and a workshop for sewing. There also are plans for a maternity clinic, workshops where various crafts can be taught, and a social hall flanked by a soccer field. "In that way they will have a place to have meetings, play sports, and relax; and they can see movies."

Echoing some criticisms I heard in Cairo, I asked Sr. Emmanuelle whether others were satisfied with merely providing aid for the ragpickers, at the risk of keeping them dependent, or whether there should be some attempt to have them take responsibility for changing their own situation. She answered me:

"We are not there yet. The problem is that these persons come from different villages and they are still afraid of one another. Up to this point it has been impossible to weld them into a unit. I am counting on the activities of the social hall to get them used to meeting with one another little by little, to discussing their problems together and creating a spirit of unity."

It is to Sr. Emmanuelle's great credit that she opened up the way. As Sr. Sarah said, "It is thanks to her that we now know about the work of the ragpickers. Now the Coptic Church, the Daughters of Mary, the priests, the deacons, the lay collaborators have taken up the challenge. The government has been alerted. There is a rebirth of hope, not only for the four thousand or so ragpickers of the slum of Azbet El Nakhl, but also for the fifty thousand ragpickers of Cairo who live in five 'colonies' near the city. It means hope as well for the others in other cities of Egypt."

Chapter 12

REFUGEES IN THAILAND AND THE U.S.A.

Ubon

The Mekong River. We are standing on the Thai side, among betel palms and mango trees. It is the season when the waters are low; the river is about thirty feet below us. The little gardens planted along the steep bank of the river will be washed away when the monsoon comes. There are some fishermen in a dugout canoe. Facing us about half a mile away there is a long, deserted beach—Laos.

You can just make out the houses set back in the trees. The village of Tha-Khek, I am told. Nothing is moving, not the slightest quiver; there is complete silence, no sign of life. The landscape is fixed in its static harmony. There is also an island—Laotian—with two Christian villages, but no trace of an inhabitant.

It is at night that the refugees cross the Mekong. They usually pay a Thai or a Laotian ferryman. "You have to know him well, otherwise you might get robbed and drowned." They also run the risk of being shot at by the communist soldiers who never hesitate to open fire on fugitives. The children are drugged so that they will not start crying and attract attention.

Refugees also cross the river on bamboo rafts, on air mattresses, or even plastic bags filled with air, or they swim. Many die in the attempt. Having once arrived in Thailand they often are put in prison to be questioned before finally being taken to a refugee camp.

I am on my way to Ubon. An irony of history: the refugees have been installed in the former munitions depot of the American airbase used by the Phantom jets when they pounded Viet Nam and the Ho Chi Minh trail. Pedal carts circulate today on the concrete roads made for bomb carriers.

Nearly forty thousand persons are crowded together in this camp. They are living in long barracks or as families in straw huts. There are craftsmen (basket weavers, cloth weavers) displaying their wares, fruit and vegetable merchants, beverage vendors. There are children selling ice cones on the streets. At first glance you would think that you were in an overcrowded village.

You would think it, if the villagers were living from their own resources and not from international aid: every morning a quarter of a cabbage and four fish are given out to feed ten persons for two days. The refugees also have a right to ten pounds of rice every ten days for adults, and half that amount for children.

You might think you were in an ordinary village, if the villagers did not have to receive authorization to leave the camp in order to work outside. (Some of the refugees are hired by local farmers.) You might think it, if the children went to school, if the young were given a professional education, if. . . . As a matter of fact this "village" is more of a dead-end street, and the main preoccupation of those who live here is to find a way of getting out.

The refugees work day and night to learn English and French—our Western countries give preferential treatment to those who speak their language. They write to friends elsewhere. They are always on the lookout for officials sent from France, America, Germany, Australia, or Canada to select a contingent of refugees.

As the missionaries bitterly observed: "Those with degrees, those with money, those with family ties, the shrewdest, are the first to leave for Europe or America; the others wait."

Many who have been kept behind barbed wire for years seem to be condemned to the camp forever. They fled communist oppression but they have not found a place where they can live as free human beings. One day Marxist propaganda may be saying to them: "Yes, see what the free world has done to you? It has made you slaves: persons who beg their bowl of rice and pass their time doing nothing."

•

The camp has a bamboo chapel. There are about a thousand Catholics here. The former bishop of Tha Khek, Bishop Pierre Bach, of the Foreign Missions of Paris, celebrates Mass every Sunday morning. After the Mass the leaders of the community meet.

"The Christians of Laos had been prepared for the day when they would have no priests. This helps them now to take responsibility."

A major problem is the continual turnover in the population of the camp. "With every wave of departure for Europe or America, there is a certain amount of confusion; then the community once again produces leaders."

There is a small group of religious who can be counted on for a lasting presence. So far as possible, the women religious do not leave Laos, but some had to cross the Mekong. One of them in all humility confided to me: "I was too afraid of the communists and so I became a danger for my companions."

"We were obliged to work in the rice paddies; otherwise we would be given nothing to eat. Then every day there was an assembly and those who had worked badly were reproved publicly. It was possible to teach catechism, though it was very difficult because the attention of the children was monopolized by the schools. The priests did not have the right to come to the village and we were watched very closely."

Another religious added: "The hardest thing in Laos is the lack of freedom. You have to live as you are told and you cannot express an opinion."

When they arrived in Thailand, the Laotian sisters were first housed in a convent in the city of Ubon. Then they were asked to go live in the refugee camp, to share the lot of their compatriots. They willingly accepted being refugees themselves, not asking permission to leave the country before their turn. Along with some lay persons, they give catechism instruction to children and adults, they work in the clinic, visit the sick and the poor, and give out clothing that church agencies have collected. For them the time spent in the camp is not lost.

New York City

At Delancey Street, you get on the M, J, or K train. You cross the East River via the Williamsburg Bridge. As you cross there is a good view of Manhattan: on the right, the United Nations building, the Empire State building and a whole panoply of skyscrapers; on the left the two towers of the World Trade Center, 110 stories high.

In Brooklyn you get off at Marcy Avenue. The old station is painted blue with a wavy yellow steak on it. Two youngsters are throwing a ball against a wall covered with designs that are more or less psychedelic. The great number of Hasidic Jews that you pass is striking.

After twenty telephone calls I finally got a half-hour interview with Fr. Brian Karvelis, pastor of Transfiguration parish. An immense energy exudes from the man. "We have an awful lot to do because we have to serve those whom no one else is serving."

His people: 65 percent from the Dominican Republic, 5 percent from Ecuador. That is, seventeen thousand immigrants out of twenty-five thousand are Catholics. Half are "illegal": they came to the United States with a short-term visa and stayed on after it had expired. Of the 30 percent who make up the rest of the parish, two-thirds are Puerto Rican. Practically then, the whole parish is Spanish-speaking. Someone said to me, "The diocese of Brooklyn is probably more a mission territory than some dioceses in the Third World."

Fr. Karvelis put it this way: "They are very poor and work at jobs that pay badly. Because they are illegal, they have no rights whatsoever. They can be exploited by anybody: their employer, their landlord—whoever. Everyone knows that they have no recourse and no protection."

Fr. Karvelis is very sensitive to the precarious situation of undocumented immigrants. He testified at a symposium on immigration: "Theirs is a life of fear and terror. They use passwords to signal the arrival of immigration officials at a factory, and they run and hide in the washrooms or elsewhere. I have parishioners who were picked up on the way to church or on their way out of the supermarket."

I was sent by Fr. Karvelis to the Southside Community Mission. It is an office that he set up to help the undocumented immigrants in his district face up to the "injustice, brutality, and inhumanity of the system in which they live." Placed under the control of the parish, the mission receives subsidies from the diocese, from the city and the state of New York, as well as from private foundations. The mission undertakes various actions with regard to official channels, tries, when possible, to normalize the situation of illegal residents, and plays the role of an employment agency. Unemployment brings with it many harmful consequences.

"The people stay at home, walk around, get bored. There are suicides. Seeing that their father doesn't work, the children lose respect for him. Some of them let themselves be taken in by easy ways of making money: prostitution, drugs, and so forth." This was the opinion of the director of the mission, a Puerto Rican.

Most of the apartment buildings are old and poorly maintained. "We get complaints from the occupants: they have no heat, their ceiling is collapsing, and the like. Then we go find the landlord and make him undertake repairs." As in other sections of the city, there are buildings set on fire, by accident or on purpose—in order to collect the insurance.

The mission has become a meeting place for those who want to study the problems facing the whole community.

"We have tenant associations in some of the apartment buildings. In banding together, a lot more can be done to improve the situation or at least make sure that it doesn't get worse."

Protest demonstrations have been organized, particularly to bring about some modicum of justice in the public school system, which, according to Fr. Karvelis, is "a total disaster." In the grammar school 55 percent of the students do not speak English, and yet there is not one bilingual teacher. The level of reading capacity is the lowest in the whole city. Classrooms are so overcrowded that the children are divided into three groups; they come to school in shifts.

The mission does not maintain a religious orientation and helps undocumented immigrants regardless of their belief. The majority of the Catholics in the parish go to church only rarely. "Nevertheless," said Fr. Karvelis, "I think that most of them are friendly toward us. We constitute for them a link—sometimes the only link—with American society."

•

"I'm tired of living like this. I *had* to come here; I planned to work in order to save money and then return to my own country. But now there is a problem. When I was in Haiti I wasn't interested at all in politics, because I didn't know anything. From here, I could see much better what was going on back there. As someone who belongs to Jesus Christ, I was obliged to take a stance openly against certain abuses. When you do that, you are exposed. Then if you go back, you run the risk of being killed or put in prison. So I have not been able to go back for two reasons: I haven't been able to save the money that I need, and I am afraid of what they might do to me because of the political stance I took."

"Your wife and two children, can't they come to New York?"

"No, my wife has tried three times already. She is always refused because I am here illegally. In order to have your family come, you have to prove that you can support them, and this is impossible because I have no right to work."

Jacques has been living for three years in Brooklyn. His father is dead and he must support not only his wife and children but his mother, his grandmother, and his younger brothers and sisters. In Haiti he could not manage it. Here he makes $124 a week as a cleaner in a factory. But he is not happy.

"Here I laugh, but it is as though I didn't laugh. I sing, but it is as though I cry. I cannot stay here very long."

Tens, maybe hundreds, of thousands of Haitians live in New York. Some are refugees for political reasons, some for economic reasons: it is not easy to draw the line. They are divided by social class and political opinion. In church, it comes to the surface in the use of Creole by some and French by others.

"A certain 'elite' of good Catholics wanted us to have elegant liturgical celebrations in French, to have a 'French' school, and so forth, but we refused. We decided that we should preach the good news to the immigrants as a single group and not establish a privileged class. Only a minority speak French whereas everyone can speak Creole. Of the eight priests who work with the Haitians in New York, five of us speak Creole."

It is a matter of choice. Someone told me about the following dialogue between a bourgeois Haitian woman and a Haitian priest.

"Father, do you say Mass in Creole?"

"Yes."

"But many don't come then."

"That's true, but then again many do come."

"Yes, but they are not the same ones."

"True, they are not the same ones."

If you opt for the poor, you run the risk of excluding the rich. But if you opt for the rich—and who would pretend that we have not done this?—it is the poor who are shunted aside.

Part Four

Repression and Liberation

Whether we like it or not, authentic preaching of the gospel necessarily brings with it political consequences, in the broad sense of the term. This is all the more obvious when the place where the gospel is preached is marked by glaring inequalities, injustices, or oppression. I have visited any number of places where human dignity is held in contempt. I am not directly concerned here with Christians or non-Christians under communist regimes. But this does not mean—and I must ask the reader to believe me—that I am any the less sensitive to communist than to capitalist exploitation.

Vincent Cosmáo has written: "Often linked with successive systems of domination throughout the centuries, the church finds itself tensed between the effort to sacralize the established order, even if it perpetuates itself by terror, and the effort to invest its energies and concern in the liberation of the poor" (*Changer le monde, une tâche pour l'Eglise,* Paris: Cerf, 1979).

To his words we can add those of Bishop Proaño, of Riobamba, Ecuador: "If we take a general survey of the reality of the church as it is in Latin America, we can say that there are two opposed attitudes: that of a rich church allied with the powerful, and that of a poor church committed to the poor" (*Concilium,* no. 150, 1979).

This dualistic reality can be found, sadly enough, throughout the Third World. I recall a conversation with a bishop who, in his anticommunist feelings, went almost to the point of justifying torture. On the other hand the Latin American bishops, meeting in Puebla, declared: "The church's prophetic denunciations and its concrete commitments to the poor have, in not a few instances, brought down persecution and oppression of various kinds upon it. The poor themselves have been the first victims of this oppression" ("Final Document," no. 1, 138).

The preaching of the gospel, the effort at conscientization, the fight for justice and respect for human rights, the struggle for the liberation of the poor, often brings with it brutal repression carried out in the name of "national security," or "the combat against atheistic communism," or simply in the name of the established order. However, as Vincent Cosmao reminds us again: "Either God makes persons free or he is not God. Those who have caught a glimpse of this . . . no longer fear any power, no longer fear death, even if they know by experience that their assurance of overcoming fear and anguish must be renewed every day"(op. cit.).

In El Salvador, I met Bishop Oscar Romero a few weeks before he was assassinated (March 24, 1980). He told me humbly and simply: "As a Christian I do not believe in death without resurrection; if they kill me, I will rise again in the people of El Salvador." Six other priests of his diocese and hundreds of lay persons had already met the same fate. Many more have been killed since then. I saw a copy of the bulletin from the archdiocese of San Salvador that gave a list of the victims of repression during the week of May 30, 1980. They included 125 *campesinos,* two laborers, twenty-eight students, three teachers, nine office workers, ten merchants, and thirty-five unknown victims.

Where is it going, all this violence that provokes a response of violence from populist organizations and urban guerrillas? I do not know. However, I also visited nearby Nicaragua where Christians participated in the overthrow of the Somoza dictatorship. They are now working to build a new Nicaragua. They took a very active part in the campaign to eradicate illiteracy during the spring and summer of 1980 and they occupy important government posts. Think of Fr. Miguel d'Escoto or Fr.

Ernesto Cardenal. They are present at the heart of the revolution, just as much as are Marxists and those of other leanings. "I am convinced that the fact of Christian participation in the revolutionary process in Nicaragua could have enormous repercussions on the church throughout Latin America," Gustavo Gutiérrez said to me in Managua. He was there to help Nicaraguan Christians reflect on the relationships between their faith and Marxism.

If—and, please God, it will not happen!—the Nicaraguan revolution becomes perverted into another totalitarian regime, this would not mean that the Christians made a mistake in having worked along with it. It would only mean that they have to continue their struggle.

Chapter 13

THE PHILIPPINES:
OF SUGAR AND MEN

We are on the island of Negros, one of the seven thousand of the Philippine archipelago. One swing of the machete to sever the cane stalk, two more to hack off the leaves. Eight hours a day under the blazing sun. Some men, with bundles of stalks on their rounded shoulders, make their way up long, inclined planks with crosspieces nailed on them—like what you see in chicken coops—and dump the bundles into a trailer.

At a short distance, twenty-five bamboo huts on piles are shoved up against one another and pushed back against a hedge of banana trees by a green wave of sugar cane that stops only a few yards from their doors. This is the compound for the permanent workers on the Lorito *hacienda* ("plantation"). The owner eliminated the little gardens cultivated by the workers so that he could plant a few extra feet of sugar cane.

"How are things going?"

"It is a life more like death. We barely subsist, in wretched conditions." They get just enough to eat—some corn, some rice, some dried fish. They dress in rags and burlap bags. We meet a man who worked on the plantation for sixty years; for his pension he gets nine pounds of rice a week. Another, who began

86

working here in 1914, gets nothing. "His children are able to take care of him," the owner explained.

Workers ask the missionary whom I accompanied to bring some clothes with him the next time he comes. He told me, "We used to do it, but I stopped because it perpetuates a beggar mentality. I give out clothing only in cases of emergency."

A little further along, the San José plantation. A water buffalo in a pond. A low, shaky hut. Inside, when my eyes get used to the darkness, I see men lying out on the bamboo floor. It is a group of *sacadas*—seasonal workers hired for the harvest. They have just finished their day's work. They lie there exhausted; they make no move as we draw near. Their empty stares show no surprise at our incongruous presence.

We manage to get into a conversation with two or three of them. One tells us that he is from Cebu, the next island. He owns a farm of about two acres. It is not enough to support his family, so he comes to work seven months a year at Negros—for a pittance.

Other plantation owners—*hacenderos*—treat their workers better. We happened to arrive at one plantation during the noon break. There was an enormous pot of rice and fish soup. A dormitory was set up in a hangar with bunk beds and even an electric bulb hanging from the ceiling. "Here, they've got a palace," said the missionary. But that "palace" was an exception.

The Philippines is the only predominantly Christian country in Asia. "Discovered" by Magellan in 1521, the Philippines are named after Philip II of Spain. In 1898 the United States took over Spain's role, until independence in 1946. "Thanks" to the Spanish colonization, more than 80 percent of the archipelago is Catholic (Islam predominates in the south).

The missionary told me: "With these men, there is no question of giving sermons. My aim is simply to give them a better self-image, to give them something to hope for. At the moment, they are not looking for the good life, just a chance to survive."

We then return to Bacolod, the capital of the province of West Negros. On the outskirts, an armed guard in a sentry box stands watch over the gate across the road. Because we are white, he lets us by. Before us, a whole series of villas ranging from comfortable to luxurious: these are the homes of *hacenderos*.

You can find similar gilded enclaves in Manila: Forbes Park, Bel Air, and others. Surrounded by high walls, these sumptuous residential districts, with lawns and flower beds and pools, shelter the privileged class. You can enter only by showing white skin. The impression is that of an entrenched camp.

The country is run by a very small elite—perhaps 1 percent of the population. They have all the power, economic as well as political. There is a middle class made up of government officials, doctors, lawyers. Then there are the masses, the poor. The rich feel threatened by the poor, who are all around them. That is why they barricade themselves in, a sociologist explained.

The rich even have a guard, twenty-four hours a day, at their family tomb located in American-style cemeteries whose large highway billboards boast of silence. But walls, guards, and vicious dogs are not the only means of defense the rich have. They have a much more subtle weapon, forged over the centuries: paternalism.

This, in effect, is what the *hacendero* of Negros says to his workers: "I own the land, you own nothing. I own the plot where your hut stands, and I own your hut. Because you have nothing, you work for me and I give you a wage insufficient to provide you with a living. Thus, you have to come to me for a bit of rice in hard times, for medicine when you are sick, for my care to assure the education of your children, for your baptisms, marriages, funerals. You are always indebted to me, and you even owe me gratitude."

Paternalism is reinforced by the *compadre* system. A tenant farmer asks his landlord to be the godfather of his child. He thus gains a certain security, but loses the freedom to express grievances against his landlord. It is not hard to see how such a situation does nothing to foster a spirit of resistance.

For a divergent view of things, I was taken to the headquarters—a wooden barracks—of the local sugar workers' union. Ed and Benilda Tejada received me there. Ed, twenty-four years old, from a wealthy family, with a degree in philosophy and political science from the Ateneo, in Manila, a Jesuit university, is the head of the union. "I began by working four months on a *hacienda,* cutting sugar cane. It was hard at the beginning, but I learned the skills. I lived on my own wages; that's very important. I was hungry. It is the only way to acquire the mentality of the workers."

All the permanent staff of the union—twenty-five persons, when I visited there—have to work several months incognito on a plantation. There are as well 125 "organizers" taken from the ranks of the workers.

The life of a unionist is not rosy. You are continually up against the implacable opposition of the *hacenderos*. Ed drew up the balance sheet: that night, five staff members in prison, including the vice-president; another killed two months earlier by a soldier (paid, it seems, by one of the owners). Ed himself was in prison forty-two days: "There were no charges against me." He still must report to the police once a week. "We are always waiting for something worse to happen," Benilda told me.

Ed and his wife have compromised a future that otherwise would have been full of promise. "Once you are known as being involved in the union, all other opportunities are closed to you." They do not harbor any illusions about a moment of triumphant vindication. "The struggle will last our whole life. We accept that."

"More than three hundred workers are deprived of their jobs because they were caught by suprise at one of our meetings." Despite all this, the union has ten thousand members. Activity is limited by martial law; strikes are forbidden.

"However, we still take certain actions, especially on the *haciendas* that are off the main roads, where the police don't like to go. For example, we cut the cane but refuse to load it until this or that grievance is met."

In this sphere a process of reeducation—conscientization—is yet to be achieved. "We talk to the workers about their living conditions, the causes behind their exploitation. They are underpaid because they are weak and have no voice. The *hacenderos* say they are lazy; this isn't true. Within the limits of their endurance, they work hard."

The Philippine landowner is not the only enemy. "We are dependent upon international politics. The economic decisions that affect life in the Philippines are not made in Manila, but in the United States. We are the victims of an imperialism that uses the feudal structures of our country. We are not communists—

not yet. But all those who concern themselves with the lot of the workers are considered to be communists."

The union was not founded by a Marxist, but by a Jesuit, Fr. Hector Mauri. "We began in 1962," he told me, "but certain church leaders thought that it would be better to preach the gospel to the rich rather than organize the poor. We had to suspend our union activity from 1964 to 1971. Evidently, during this time the rich didn't undergo a conversion: the workers' situation had become remarkably worse."

I was told that for a long time the church in the Philippines avoided social questions on the principle of the distinction between the temporal and spiritual domains. "It is only since Vatican II that people are interested in these problems." The church is a powerful institution: ninety bishops, four thousand five hundred priests, seven thousand religious, five thousand schools, a dozen universities. It carries a grave responsibility.

Today, faced with the dictatorship of President Marcos, in power since 1965, faced with the martial law declared in 1972, the majority of the bishops, under the leadership of Cardinal Sin, hold to the principle of "critical collaboration" with the state. A minority has thrown in its lot with the regime; at the other extreme, another minority refuses all collaboration (see the dossier in *Informations Catholiques Internationales,* no. 547, February 1980).

Fr. Mauri is Italian. He is assisted by Fr. Edgar Saguinsin, a Filipino from a well-to-do family in Negros. Fr. Saguinsin's brother runs one of the island's sugar factories. He himself is pastor of a local parish, and he has had his difficulties with the *hacenderos.* "One Sunday, before the imposition of martial law, I invited three of the strikers to mount the pulpit at the time for the sermon. Since then, many landowners don't come to Mass. They are trying to cut me off economically: the Sunday collection is down by half; donations for the catechists are down by three-quarters."

Fr. Saguinsin was supposed to have been arrested, but he was away the night the police broke in. Christians who are active in the labor movement are often among the victims of police and military action. They are accused of promoting communist subversion (there has been a Maoist guerrilla war raging for ten years in the Philippines). This charge is not always true. Nevertheless there are Christians who have chosen—as has happened in other countries—to work with Marxists.

"We respect their views, but ours are a little different," Fr. Saguinsin told me. "We think that before any revolution, the workers have to be given their dignity. As it is now, they are domesticated and a prey to fatalism. We have to help them get free of these evils."

Chapter 14

SOUTH KOREA: SHANTIES vs. DOGHOUSES

Saturday afternoon in a village in South Korea. Choun Ja ("the daughter of spring"), a pretty twenty-one-year-old girl, has just returned from the spinning mill. As is the case with many young persons from the country, she left her small village four years earlier to come to work in the city. I wait while she freshens up and has something to eat; she left the house at six o'clock that morning without having eaten anything.

"They give us a breakfast at the factory but I don't eat it, because the food is unfit to eat. They give us rice which is either burnt or pasty and soup which is either watery or too salty."

Choun Ja lives in a private home but many of her companions live in the dormitories provided by the factory; they have to be satisfied with the food served there. At Masan, in the southern part of the country, I visited a sort of youth hostel that houses six thousand young girls. There are eight each in a room thirteen feet long and nine feet wide. Luckily there is no furniture to take up space: everyone sleeps on mats.

Choun Ja comes home very vivacious and happy despite the six hours she spent today in front of her machine and its infernal racket. "I have to tie the threads together and put the bobbins in their cylinders. You have to know how to do it and move very quickly; otherwise the thread, especially the synthetic varieties, will cut your fingers off."

She shows me a gash near her nail. She is free now until ten o'clock Sunday night. Then she will work the whole night through. "Oh, yes, we are sleepy but the woman overseer stops us from going to sleep." She will get home again Monday morning about nine o'clock and will have to return to the mill at two o'clock that afternoon. "It is really very hard. Everybody hates that schedule and it repeats itself every three weeks."

Choun Ja seldom has a full day off. "They tell us to take one when there is less work." If she has not been absent from work for an entire year, she has the right to a week of paid vacation in order to go visit her parents. The company for which Choun Ja works is, comparatively speaking, quite generous to its personnel. In a number of factories the work day is twelve hours long and there are only two days off per month.

Wages are extremely low. By refusing herself anything but the basic necessities, Choun Ja manages to save a little money, with a view toward marriage. I asked her if she felt she was being exploited. "It seems to me that the company thinks only of its own profit and not the good of the workers. It is impossible to improve working conditions and anyone who tries something is fired right away. We are even forbidden to speak among ourselves."

There is a union in the mill but it inspires no confidence in the workers, because it is tied in with the management of the company.

"We have no power; we are kept isolated from one another. The girls refuse to get involved because they know that they will spend only a few years at the factory and then they will go back home to their villages."

Somebody said to me that a woman twenty-five or thirty years old would have a very difficult time getting a job because management would be afraid of her. "They prefer the young girls from the country who are still ignorant and compliant."

Despite all this, Choun Ja is in the process of forming a team of Young Christian Workers in order to try to create some unity and friendship among the factory girls. "It is hard and I often feel like giving up but I am a disciple of Christ and I know that the apostles also became discouraged."

The Young Christian Workers and their Protestant counterpart, the Urban and Industrial Mission, were playing a discreet but effective role when I visited South Korea. Their efforts attracted the suspicions of a government anxious to avoid the least grain of sand in the gears of the Korean "economic miracle." Both groups were under close surveillance—an agent of the Korean version of the CIA visited the YCW headquarters every day—and pressure was brought to bear on the more active members.

"We are carrying out underground activities about which we cannot talk very much," they told me at the YCW. They were helping the workers become aware of their rights.

•

"The higher up you go, the poorer it gets." The little stone houses and the huts cling to the desolate mountain. We walk across a plank over an open sewer ditch and now we are climbing a steep path. There are forty-six thousand persons in this shantytown, Si Heung, a half-hour taxi ride from the center of Seoul.

Koreans from other parts of the country move close to the capital city, where there are already eight million inhabitants, with the hope of finding a job or in order to give a boy the chance to study (the Koreans are willing to make enormous sacrifices to send their children to school). They rent a hut and try to survive.

It is hard during the winter, when subzero days are not uncommon and the house is made only of wooden planks. "Families have frozen to death." It is hard too in the summer, when typhus is on the rampage. It is hard when the water in the well has been contaminated by somebody with tuberculosis. Promiscuity, lack of hygiene, lack of food—they all conspire to crush you.

In 1976 in another shantytown the authorities—as they do periodically—undertook the demolition of a certain number of "illegal houses." Sixteen families, victims of the government enterprise, found tents for themselves, one of which served as a chapel. They had begun to relate to a certain Protestant group who had agreed to help them. The police came, knocked down the chapel tent, and carried it off in a truck. A few days later the tents in which the families were living met the same fate. The families found another shack but it too was destroyed. They then went back into another tent; it was torn down and confiscated. A statement of protest was drawn up, and I want to quote an extract:

"The dogs owned by the rich and the important have the privilege of having their own houses. They are treated better than are human beings without means. If you were to look for somebody to go knock down the doghouses of the rich, chances are you wouldn't find anyone who would do it. Even those who knock down huts and tents where humans are living would shake with fear and would never destroy a doghouse that belongs to the head of a city district or the mayor of the city itself. But there are those who are not afraid to destroy houses where human beings live and, even more unthinkable, places used as churches."

A few weeks later, at the end of an ecumenical service celebrated in the cathedral of Seoul, a Protestant woman, Lee Woo Jung, read out a declaration demanding a return to democracy. Grave sin! Eighteen persons, including priests, pastors, and well-known and respected citizens such as the former president of the republic, Yoon Po Sun, and the leader of the opposition, Kim Dae Jung, were arrested and given heavy prison sentences. It was the incident concerning the tents, which we have just related, that inspired a Protestant pastor, along with his friends, to draw up the statement. The regime of President Park Chung Hee could not tolerate such an act of rebellion.

Among the thirty-seven million South Koreans there are about three and a half million Protestants and one million Catholics; they are divided politically. Some, because of their anticommunist stance, supported Park Chung Hee; others take refuge behind a prudent reserve. A bishop said to me: "If our activities are purely religious, the government does not inhibit us; on the contrary it helps us. Only those who get involved in politics have problems."

One of the eighteen arrested "rebels" said: "Most persons are afraid, and that is human enough. Only a minority is ready to struggle desperately and to agree to the sacrifices that are necessary."

One of the leading figures in this struggle for justice and re-spect for human rights is Cardinal Stephen Kim, the archbishop of Seoul. He explained:

"The church's mission is to preach the good news and to preach it first of all to the poor. This means that the church must be present among the poor, in the slums and in the factories, and serve the poor there. This essential note of Christianity has too often been neglected by our people and even by our clergy. On the other hand when Christians begin to show that they are aware of this mission of the church, they come up against the authorities. Actually, the problems of the poor often have so-cietal roots. When this is seen clearly, citizens are led to oppose the policies of the government—not the government itself but its policies."

This results in political repression. One of the most famous victims of the Park regime is the poet Kim Chi Ha. He was con-demned to death for being a communist on the basis of admis-sions forced from him. He now is stagnating in jail.

In October 1979 Park Chung Hee was assassinated by the head of the Korean secret service. After a brief period of libera-lization, the army took over the reins of power. In May 1980 it crushed the insurrection in the village of Kwangju, killing hun-dreds of persons. The struggle continues. . . .

Chapter 15

ZIMBABWE:
LOSSES AND GAINS

At one o'clock in the morning a band of armed men came to the mission at Berejena, in Zimbabwe, formerly called Rhodesia. They assembled all the boarders at the secondary school for a session of antireligious propaganda. The students began to suspect that the band was not composed of true guerrilla freedom-fighters. After a short while some of the men got Fr. Killian out of bed and brought him to the place where the session was being held. The bibles had been piled up in a corner. When he saw that they were going to burn them, Fr. Killian rose up. They immediately shot him dead.

Fr. Killian Hüsser, a Swiss priest of the Society of Bethlehem, was killed on February 19, 1980. Will we ever know who his murderers were? Was it a dissident group of guerrillas? Was it some Africans in the pay of whites who wanted to cast a shadow on the guerrilla movement just before the elections, or who wanted to "punish" the church? There is no definitive proof for any of these hypotheses.

Fr. Killian's murder is not the only one to remain unclarified. In all, twenty missionaries, including one local priest, were killed during the conflict. Two others disappeared and are considered dead; four lay missionaries were also killed. Some of them were apparently killed by guerrillas; others, no doubt, were killed at the instigation of those in favor of the regime then in power. In

addition, thirty-six priests and religious, including Bishop Donal
Lamont of Umtali, were either arrested, imprisoned, or ex-
pelled. This is what the war cost the Catholic Church alone.

It was not the first time that the mission of Berejena, located
on an African reservation, the Chibi Tribal Trust Land, was
affected by the prevailing hostilities. In 1976 Fr. Paul Egli was
imprisoned for having had contacts with the guerrillas. Later, an
army detachment was stationed at Berejena. It was attacked by
guerrillas. The African priest who was located in that area was
also arrested then.

•

The blue, purple, and red blossoms on the trees are so many
splashes of color against the gray sky. There are shell marks in
my room. The church was damaged as well the night that Fr.
Killian was murdered. Today the man responsible for this important mission is Fr. Franz Camenzind. He spent most of the war
in this region.

"Seven hundred persons lived right here: the students and
professors at the school, the sick and the personnel of the hospital, the sisters and the priests. We missionaries were under con-
stant surveillance by the army. They were looking for grounds to
put us in prison. Many persons were beaten and even tortured in
order to obtain some sort of evidence that would compromise
us. But the people always defended us."

Though it was dangerous to go about, the missionaries made
efforts to keep in contact with the communities dispersed in the
bush. "Every time there was some sort of military engagement
we tried to get to that place in order to see what had happened,
to treat the wounded and bury the dead." In October 1976 the
little truck belonging to the mission was exploded by a mine.
After that nobody took that road.

"When we had things to transport we used carts drawn by
donkeys. We ourselves moved about by bicycle. We left the car
out on the paved state road, which was kept open by the army."

In contrast to many other missions, the mission at Berejena
continued its activities during most of the war, though not
without risks. Fr. Camenzind told me, "One day I came out on

my motorbike at the spot where a mine had just gone off. The soldiers were furious and nearly executed me then and there."

•

The smooth black mountains look like whales riding the swell of the green trees. As we drove along we could still make out the charred remains of the burnt-out huts. "When a mine went off the army burned everything in the area. The people finally went and hid themselves in the bush. They are starting to come out now."

A chapel stands at the crossroads. This is the station of Ngundu that depends on the mission of Berejena. Ten communities are attached to this station but two of them were scattered by the war. Today we are at the monthly meeting of the leaders of these communities. They are arriving by foot, by bicycle, and by bus from an area thirty-seven miles in diameter.

They begin by warming up the tom-toms and then singing. Next the program for the month is planned, the money collected at the harvest feast is given over to the priest, and the places are chosen where Mass will be celebrated during the week (for example, in the home of a family where someone is sick).

The leaders had brought with them three chickens and some corn for the meal. During the war it was the priest who provided the meal but now the communities must once again be able to take care of themselves. The women (seven out of fourteen persons) prepared the *tsa-tsa*, a sort of corn gruel, which makes up the basis of the diet, and they cooked the chickens. We were served with the great courtesy and thoughtfulness that is a characteristic of the Shona people.

I had a conversation with Brito, the catechist of Ngundu. Every Tuesday he leaves his wife and eight children in order to make the circuit of the communities, returning home again on Sunday night. In Fr. Camenzind's estimation, "He does the same work as a priest, except of course for saying Mass." Brito followed a full-time training course for two years. It was in large part due to his perfect knowledge of the area that contact with the thousand or so Catholics who live there was maintained during the war.

"The Christians wrote to me asking me to come visit them, and I went and brought communion to them. I went nearly everywhere except in the zones that were too dangerous."

"Still, it was quite risky, wasn't it?"

"Yes, I was afraid of the soldiers, but as a matter of fact I was never really in danger. And when someone wrote to me, I could not stop myself from going. . . ." One can imagine the anxiety his family went through!

During all of this, the Christians were reluctant to move out. They were extremely busy as well. "You always had to be ready to help the guerrillas and as a result it wasn't possible to spend every Sunday morning in church. Or maybe one member of the family was delegated to go. This is how some persons lost the habit of practicing their religion."

Another factor tended to reinforce the increasingly perceptible estrangement. The catechist told me: "The guerrillas organized meetings in the villages at night. They cried out slogans such as 'Down with the Bible!,' 'Down with the church!' But there were also combatants who went to Mass."

Trained in China and based in socialist Mozambique, many of the ZANLA guerrillas had undergone a Marxist indoctrination, whereas those of ZIPRA were influenced by Russia and by other countries of Eastern Europe. (These two groups were led by Robert Mugabe and Joshua Nkomo, respectively.) Some of these guerrillas tried to impart their ideology to the noncombatants with whom the war put them in contact. "They told us that the church was linked to the colonialists."

Historically speaking, the charge is not entirely without foundation, even if the Christian schools made a considerable contribution—often without willing it—to the formation of the African nationalists. I asked Fr. Camenzind if the influence of this anti-Christian propaganda could still be felt and he answered in the affirmative: "The people don't say it outright but it appears clearly, especially among the young." This was confirmed by some of the teachers at Berejena: "They were troubled by the slogans and now fewer of them go to church."

"It was also stated that Christianity is the religion of the whites, and some guerrillas tried to revitalize the traditional religion, especially the cult of the anscestors," Fr. Camenzind added. "In this domain the Catholic Church is not in a bad position, because we had already integrated certain elements of belief in the ancestors within our liturgy even before the war."

Another example of the Africanization of the liturgy would be prayers for rain. We are on the trail that leads to Maramba. Fr. Camenzind regularly covers the twelve miles that separate the village from this mission by bicycle. "We discovered the importance of utilizing means that were in keeping with the resources possessed by our people. They cannot afford to pay for the gasoline that a car would need."

A small white chapel in the bush. The roof had been stripped by someone who wanted the tiles, but the guerrillas ordered him to put them back. The faithful are already assembled. They are all country people. Catholics are but a minority in the region.

After the liturgy of the word we go in procession to a dry field swept by the wind. There are songs and prayers, and then the priest sprinkles the land with holy water at the four extremities of the compass. When we return to the chapel he blesses the seeds that have been left at the foot of the altar in tin containers painted white, in bottles, and in bowls.

In the morning we had prayed for rain at Berejena as well, but with a little more ceremony. Three women carried gourds of water on their heads. We stopped at three different fields. Each time after a reading from the Bible and a long dialogue with an elder of the community, one of the women sprinkled the ground around her and then carried out a dance accompanied by the trills of the women's voices. The real goal of such a ceremony is perhaps not so much that of making rain come as of recognizing that it is a gift from God.

At the end of the Mass some lay persons address the group, to impart news and announcements. "They are the ones who direct the community." And then a gesture that both surprised and touched us: a collection was taken up for the visitors. The money collected enabled us to buy some hard-boiled eggs and bananas for our noonday meal at a bus stop as we were returning to town.

•

At the archbishop's house in Gwelo, the diocese in which Bere-jena is sited, Fr. Elsener told me: "Generally speaking, even if they were not in favor of the war, our missionaries felt sympathy for the cause of the African nationalists. Though we tried to remain neutral, we were in a certain way on the side of the guerrillas even if this meant only bringing them medical aid. The whites looked upon us as traitors." Nearly the whole of the African population supported the guerrillas, and the priests who served the Africans had a tendency to identify themselves with them. This distinguished them from some of their confreres who were working in white parishes.

All foreigners were free to leave the country but very few did so. "Collectively we had decided to remain where we were in order to share in the sufferings of the people. In addition, we were able to bring help to others and the simple fact of our presence constituted for them a sort of protection: we were there to denounce injustices."

The diocese of Gwelo, and in this it was not alone, took up a position that was particularly clear. Toward the end of the war it was the position of the Catholic Church in Zimbabwe in general, as can be seen by the attitude of Bishop Lamont and many declarations of the episcopacy and the diocesan Justice and Peace Commission.

Nevertheless, as one would expect, the whole spectrum of possible attitudes was present. This included, notably among some of the elderly missionaries who were gripped by a fear of communism, a quasi-identification with the cause of the whites. Some even carried arms or surrounded their mission with barbed wire; this was especially true in the diocese of Bulawayo.

Still, Fr. Elsener was able to affirm that, generally speaking, the Catholic Church was on the side of the people.

•

If the greater part of the missions in the diocese of Gwelo were able, at least partially, to continue their activities during the war, the same cannot be said of areas that had to be abandoned by the priests and religious. About fifty primary and secondary schools, a dozen hospitals and dispensaries, some minor seminaries and novitiates were closed either by order of the army or under pressure from the guerrillas. Often the buildings suffered considerable damage.

In those places where the church was able to continue, one could observe a deepening of the relationship between it and the local people. Fr. Camenzind told me in this regard:

"The war made us understand that we could not exist without being supported by the people. Like them we were exposed to all the dangers. A greater poverty helped us as well to share better in their situation. Though we rendered service to them, we also needed them. Each morning our first preoccupation was to find out what happened during the night. Before going anywhere we had to ask advice in order to know whether it would be possible and sensible."

Fr. Elsener stressed the fact that when a group of guerrillas came into a new area they sought information from the local people. The fate of the missionaries depended on the opinion the people had of them.

I asked Fr. Camenzind if he still saw signs of that greater closeness between the church and the people.

"Especially here at Berejena, the fact that one of us was killed has left its mark on the people. They came to understand that we are here in Zimbabwe not for ourselves but for them. This has strengthened the community, and still remains an important factor. With regard to the practice of their religion, we have surely lost many Christians, but we have acquired a huge number of friends because of the fact that we lived through the same difficulties that they did."

Chapter 16

EL SALVADOR: BASE COMMUNITIES UNDER FIRE

Furious, the minibus throws itself against the paved road that rises constantly before us almost like a wall. We are on our way from the market town of Chalatenango, the capital of the department of the same name, driving toward the plateau near the Honduran border. Standing, or rather bent over in two because of the vehicle's low roof, there is hardly space to put your feet. It took us two and a half hours of jolts and dust to cover the nineteen miles.

The bus sets us down at the foot of a steep hill. Somewhat groggy I can still hear the shrill cries of the women who at each bus stop were selling *pupusas* (a sort of pancake covered with beans or white cheese) and oranges. Short of breath we climb amid the sweet-smelling grass. Finally, behind a screen of bamboo and banana trees, we see a house with thick mud walls and a tile roof.

We go through a courtyard where two or three small pigs are running loose and come to a smaller yard being swept by a young girl. Her mother is there also. She has had twelve children, two of whom are dead. As is the case with nearly all the able-bodied men of the region, the father of the family and the two sons who still live at home have gone off to harvest coffee.

It is a six-hour bus ride from here and they will not be home again for two or three months.

Many of the peasants, and my hosts are no exception, do not own any land. Every year they rent a tiny plot where they struggle to grow corn and beans, with a machete and pruning hook their only tools. They have to use fertilizers; otherwise the soil, steeply sloped, eroded, and exhausted, yields nothing. Their harvest is carefully kept in a room smoked to prevent vermin and spoilage. It will just about suffice to feed them during the coming year.

Around October the peasants with no land go to look for work on a *finca* ("plantation"), where coffee, cotton, or cane sugar are grown. Sometimes they have to borrow money for the trip. If the wife remains home with the youngest children, she is often left with no money at all. She does not even have enough to buy medicine in case of need. "It can happen that children die for lack of proper care."

I shared a midday meal in a cotton field belonging to the Guirolas, one of the famous fourteen families—maybe there are more than fourteen now—who have always shared among them the wealth of the country. Each worker was given two tortillas—only one for children up to ten years of age, who were helping their parents—a handful of beans, and a pinch of salt.

"The beans are dirty and of poor quality and you have cockroaches and other insects for seasoning!"

The meal is the same morning and evening. There is never meat or fish. The workers eat standing, in three or four minutes; then they return to the fields with their stomachs still empty. This simple scene, in a countryside graced by sunlight and a stone's throw from the Pacific Ocean, told me more than a thousand speeches could have about the origins of the violence that is tearing the country apart.

Those who harvest the cotton suffer from the heat, the mosquitoes, and marlaria. On the coffee plantations, at higher altitudes, workers sleep in the cold at night under the trees or a tiny plastic shelter. "Very often we get sick, but we keep on working, even with a fever."

After the harvest, when they return home, they are exhausted. A woman confided to me: "I am sometimes afraid that my husband will never be able to work again." The men, if they have not spent all their money on alcohol—and who would throw the first stone at them?—bring back enough to pay for the rent of the plot of land, buy some medicine and some clothing for their family, and that is just about as far as it stretches.

As they were telling me about the life conditions of the *campesinos,* the local Christian community was assembling. Usually there are more persons present, two hundred perhaps. Today, because of the absence of those who have gone to work on the *fincas,* the congregation is composed mostly of women, children, and old men. They are seated in the courtyard of our hosts, on benches or tree trunks. The men hold their hats in their hands; their machetes lie beside them.

I look at them, bronzed faces with a stubble of beard, eyes red and watery. These are faces of the outdoors, of suffering, of fatigue. They are also faces made intent by reflection, by the desire to understand. A Mexican religious, Sr. Nico, conducts the meeting. She reads the introduction to the document drawn up by the Latin American bishops at Puebla.

What is it that characterizes Latin America? The *campesinos* give their opinion: "Those of us who work the land are the ones who do not eat, who have no medicine to take care of themselves, who do not know how to read or write. Those who don't work are the ones who eat and have the best medicine."

They express themselves slowly but with great clarity. Each one of their words is carefully weighed.

In this parish there are seven communities like this one and others are being formed. Before the creation of these communities the practice of the faith was restricted to a traditional Catholicism based on popular religiosity. Bishop Luís Chávez, the predecessor of Bishop Oscar Romero as archbishop of San Salvador, began a new pastoral approach in keeping with Vatican II and Medellín.

The first task was to form leaders taken from among the people: the *celebradores* ("celebrators," "ministers") of the word. There are now thirty such leaders, men and women, in this area we are visiting. Their role was defined by one of them: "to proclaim the kingdom of God and fight against the injustices in which we are involved." The *celebradores* little by little built up the nuclei of the new communities.

These communities are very well organized. They meet regularly for discussions and celebrations. They have various committees to promote literacy, health, mutual aid ("we share our corn and beans when a family is hungry"), to smooth over disputes in the family and elsewhere, to look out for the security of the group.

Sr. Nico said: "The church has something to say in the history of the world. If it stays up in the clouds it will not fulfil its role. It must bring about liberation in every dimension."

The celebration continues. There is a hymn taken from the Nicaraguan *Misa Campesina*: "You are the God of the poor, the God who is human and simple. . . ." This is followed by the reading of the gospel, the prayer of the faithful, another song, and the celebration is ended. Sr. Nico hugs a woman and whispers to her: "The community gives strength." The woman is the mother of Faustino and Santiago Ayala. The first of them has been missing since June 1979; the other was found a few weeks ago, decapitated.

•

The Christian communities—though they are not the only ones—are the target of open persecution. The first reason for this is because at the heart of these communities a process of conscientization is going on. "We are showing the *campesinos* that the exploitation of humans by humans does not correspond to God's plan and that we have to go from an inhuman situation to one that is more human."

Another reason for the persecution is that some members of these communities have been led to give concrete expression to their faith through political commitments (and there are others who come to the faith having begun with a political commitment). At the beginning of the 1970s two orgainzations took shape to gather together the *campesinos* who had decided to fight for greater justice. They were the Christian Federation of the Landworkers of El Salvador (FECCAS) and the Union of Farm Workers (UTC). The church supported the Christians who, along with non-Christians, became involved in this type of activity.

However, not the *whole* church went in this direction. In 1978 the four conservative bishops of the country, out of a total of six, going against the position taken up by Archbishop Romero, demanded of priests and religious that they abstain from any direct or indirect collaboration with the FECCAS or the UTC.

Some young organizers of the UTC join us. One of them tells us, "My mother and my four brothers died of malnutrition." While drinking a sort of coffee made from roasted corn—those who harvest real coffee do not have enough money to buy it— they tell me about their activities:

"The most important thing is to raise the consciousness of the people, to get them to understand the national reality, and then to get them to do something. We gather the landworkers in small groups, along with leaders chosen by themselves. We organize meetings and demonstrations. Our objective is to change society. We want socialism, but a Christian socialism, because we are Christian."

Both the UTC and the FECCAS belong to the Popular Revolutionary Front, one of the populist organizations of El Salvador that espouse Marxist-Leninist doctrine. This does not mean that the *campesinos* adhere to such an ideology or even that they know what it is. The fact that they belong, however, provides the pretext for those who have economic and political power, for the army, for the so-called security forces, for groups of the extreme right to wreak the most violent repression against the members of these groups.

The community that welcomed us had been hard hit. Besides the two Ayala brothers, one of whom had been an organizer for the UTC, Ernesto Menjivar, also of the UTC, had disappeared. A *celebrador* of the word, sixty-year-old Meliton Martínez had been assassinated. "He was killed because of his Christian commitment. Because he taught the gospel, he was considered subversive."

Another *celebrador* told me how they searched his house, that of his son, and that of his daughter, how they took out clothes and burned them. "Luckily I had hidden the Bible," he added.

And so it happens in El Salvador—and elsewhere—that the word of God has become subversive.

The meeting had to discuss the temporary expulsion of Sr. Nico and one of her companions, and the false accusations brought against her. And it is not without anguish that I think of all that could have happened to them since I left El Salvador. As one of the *campesinos* remarked: "There is no freedom except for oppression."

They live in fear. Just a few minutes ago, during the celebration, we heard gunshots; they were getting closer. Faces were frozen. Then one of the UTC organizers left us in a hurry saying, "They are looking for me." Often the men go to sleep somewhere outside their houses, in hiding places, for fear of being arrested.

Another *campesino* remarked: "It's even dangerous to go to church or to the meetings of the community."

Not everybody has this courage, this heroism. Some are pulling away from the church. Sr. Nico admitted: "In the old days religion was a purely spiritual affair and didn't touch on the realities of everyday life. Now many are scandalized; they want a church like the one they used to have."

We have had a bad night, listening for suspicious noises. It is not impossible that the National Guard would make a raid while we are in the area.

"Fear is normal and if I were to say that I wasn't afraid it would be a lie," Sr. Nico confided. "But once that obstacle is overcome there remains the joy of working for the liberation of a people through evangelization."

The next day we leave for the market town of Arcatao. It is the center for the parish that was confided to Sr. Nico and the other two Mexican religious. A chaplain comes from Chalatenango every two weeks if things are calm; otherwise less frequently. Today there will be the first Mass in two months. Sr. Nico told me when there was no priest everyone gathered in the church to hear the sermons of Bishop Romero on the radio.

The priest at the altar tells the people, "Since I was here last, you have had hard times." And then he reads off the names of the parishioners who have been killed.

We pray for the dead parishioners. All of a sudden we hear some explosions and I jump. But it is only firecrackers. Just in front of the church is the market place; on the far side is the sisters' convent, which serves as a rectory. It also houses a dispensary. Unfortunately, the religious do not live there right now. It is too dangerous: the main door of the convent is just opposite the headquarters of the National Guard.

The church building is not finished yet. Most of the faithful are dressed very poorly. Some have sandals made out of old rubber tires, others have no shoes at all. A barefoot church— that is what is going to save the world.

•

Along the road all you can see is a spread of tin roofs. Above them rises the *Metrocentro,* a luxurious commercial complex, with shining Christmas balls hanging from plastic fir trees, and all the allurements of the consumer soceity. Next, all the hotels of the famous international chains. Shamefacedly, Tutunichapa hides its destitution and open wounds along the bank of a ravine: its shaky huts, its filth where dirt-black pigs rummage.

The *tugurio* ("shantytown"), one of the many scattered throughout San Salvador, houses six or seven hundred families. At the bottom of the ravine there is a fetid stream. These are the sewer waters from San Benito, San Francisco, Escalon, the upper-class districts of the capital city. A few months earlier a storm swelled the open sewer; the shacks close to the bottom of the ravine were flooded.

At the entrance to Tutunichapa the local residents' committee had hung a banner that reads, "We demand drinking water, medical assistance, electricity, and the legalization of our land occupation"—things they lack. And they could have added "work and decent salaries."

The women take in laundry, hire themselves out as domestics, sell vegetables or tortillas in the market place. The children shine shoes or sell the *Prensa Gráfica* or the *Diario de Hoy*—the newspapers of the oligarchy. The men work on construction sites or in the factories, but many of them are out of work. "We have all sorts here," Marietta told me, "workers, thieves, prostitutes."

But above all there is suffering: "I never got a chance to study; all I know is suffering," she added.

Marietta had been a seamstress in one of the large factories. "They paid us the minimum and we never had a vacation. You could go to the toilet only once during the morning. If you wanted a bite of candy, you had to hide your face behind a piece of cloth and slip it into your mouth quickly." Marietta took sick and now she works at home.

Naomi is my guide along the paths of Tutunichapa. A volcano—that is the best way I can describe for you this tiny effervescent woman, impetuous and always animated by a kind of joy. She belongs to a pastoral team made up of two Belgian priests and five "sisters" (I call them that for the sake of simplicity; their status is somewhat special).

This team is responsible for three parishes. Naomi works especially in three marginal areas (in addition to her job as secretary in the diocesan chancery). She is the "pastor" of Tutunichapa. She explained to me how one goes about forming an ecclesial base community.

"You begin by visiting each house in the area. This takes about two or three months. We consider this work to be of the greatest importance. The residents have no awareness of being worth anything. The fact that we go to them in their homes shows them that they have some worth."

Some anonymous outsiders threatened to set the whole slum on fire because it mars the appearance of the surrounding areas. A whole system of nightwatches was organized for two weeks. Naomi took part in this, along with some of the young "delinquents." "I wasn't afraid, because the people love me." The result: the formation of a youth group.

In one of the houses—because there was no other place for it—there is given a course in the basics of the Christian life, not abstract but rooted in the daily life of the people. Those who will become leaders are given a more advanced biblical training. There are also preparation sessions for those who wish to be baptized.

"Very often the ones who come are those who have lost all contact with religion. But when the prostitutes, the drunkards, the thieves, and the drug addicts turn to the Lord they make extraordinary Christians. Once they have been converted, they are told to go out and proclaim the word of God to others."

These are the Christians who are invited to make up their cell of the church. At Tutunichapa the community comprises eighty adults, plus the children.

What about politics? "Those who want to," said Naomi, "get involved in a populist organization. We ask them only that they do this as Christians and that they act as a leaven within these organizations. We try to help them to analyze situations for themselves and not let themselves be manipulated."

Such commitments, of course, draw down upon the base communities bitter criticism. One of the Belgian priests, Fr. Louis, responded this way:

"Our objective is pastoral, not political. Nevertheless, on the basis of their faith, little by little our people discover that they have a political role to play. We show them then that the more involved you get in this area, the more attentive you have to be to your own personal life, the life of your family, and your life in the community. Our role is to support and accompany the local Christians on every level of their life."

I asked Naomi if Christians could belong to right-wing organizations. "Then they would no longer be Christians," she said with a touch of roguishness. "There is respect for pluralism without taking sides with either the oligarchy or the junta. Most of our people are poor and cannot identify with the goals of the junta but rather with the revolutionary goals of the people's organizations."

With deep conviction, Fr. Louis told me: "If you want to understand the poor, you have to live at their side. Those who suffer and those who don't suffer read the word of God very differently. Their political analysis is different too."

"Let's go!" Naomi sticks her head in the window and announces a meeting. She asks the news of this one and that, and then moves on. "Let's go!" A woman is doing her wash at the fountain, which is surrounded by bamboo and palm trees. It is there that we meet a daughter of Oscar López, one of the leaders of the shantytown residents' committee. He disappeared six months earlier and no one had any hope of seeing him alive again. He was the father of five children aged six to eighteen. It was a neighbor who lived just across from the slum who denounced him. In reprisal the neighbor was executed.

We pass by the house of "Champito," a twenty-two-year-old man who was killed a few weeks earlier while carrying food to some workers at a factory on strike. Naomi told me he was one the best young men in the community. His mother shows us his photo. He was a construction worker and had completed a course in technical designing. He belonged to a workers' organization.

One of the priests of the pastoral team, Octavio Ortiz, was also assassinated in 1979. Repression and fear stymie the development of the base communities. "The propaganda says that we are communists." Nevertheless, committed Christians are not giving up the struggle.

"The people have always suffered. You don't die only from bullets; you die of hunger, of destitution, of oppression. Today the people prefer to die fighting."

•

It is Christmas in Tutunichapa. Everyone is crowded in the community hall, which is decorated with paper garlands. Instead of a Christmas tree there are palm branches and on them hang framed photos. There is one of Oscar López, another of Champito. There is a photo of Octavio Ortiz and of the other priests who have been assassinated. The following year they must have added one of Archbishop Romero, and of how many others who were in the room that night?

Fr. Louis and his companions celebrate Mass. "Christmas brings a liberating message to our earth where so many are exploited and live in misery. God willed to be born in the shantytowns of San Salvador. He tells each one of us present here that we are the ones he prefers. He teaches us how to build a world where there will be more justice and fellowship."

No, the gospel is not the opium of the people but a two-edged sword. "The word of God judges our society." The children of the shantytown reenact the search of Joseph and Mary, wandering around Bethlehem looking for a place to stay. This scene, so well known, so taken for granted, was like a whip in my face.

"Good evening, we are looking for a place to stay," a ten-year-old Joseph said to me. And when I could only answer him, "There isn't any room," an eight-year-old Mary hurled back at me this terrible indictment: "While the rich celebrate Christmas with luxurious presents, pleasure trips in Europe or North America, with banquets, the poor go hungry, live in ignorance, suffer a thousand evils, have no roof over their heads, no drinking water!"

The poor, the thieves, the prostitutes, the drug addicts (the youth of Tutunichapa announced that Christmas would be celebrated without marijuana), the tortured, the victims of repression, the assassinated prophets, will all enter the kingdom of God ahead of us.

Nevertheless, despite the sorrow and the suffering, it is laughter that finally melts this night at Tutunichapa. The shantytowners are singing and clapping their hands. I share with you this one refrain, which comes from neighboring Nicaragua, recently freed from the dictatorship of Somoza: "A joyous Christmas, with justice and freedom. A joyous Christmas in a world that is better without destitution or oppression!"

Epilogue

FAITH IS THE WORLD
IN ITS YOUTH

by Robert Masson

Throughout these pages we have been visiting the land of
faith. This land is our planet seared by the fire that Christ came
to ignite twenty centuries ago. It is true that for a long time
Christianity had been able to appear before the world as a rather
provincial thing. It had taken over the West, consolidated its
extensions into the Americas, and seemed to be content at that.
Islam, Buddhism, and the other religions of Asia and Africa
shared among themselves the soul of the other continents.

Of course the effort of Christian missionaries never ceased
coaxing the church beyond its narrow frontiers. From the very
beginning the disciples of Jesus Christ were pressed to go to the
very limits of the world and the limits of their own energies. A
ground swell forced us outside our walls during the nineteenth
century and the first part of the present century. Then things
settled down again and the wave of Western imperialism flowed
back over the scene.

The very notion of mission suffered because of the guilt feelings that were attached to Western colonization. What right did
we have to go and impose our way of life and our form of belief
and to create a situation that served to demobilize the resources
of those to whom we preached? In addition, we came up against
failures—failures that we still have not analyzed in full. What
happened in China is a good example of what I mean. Much has
been written to explain what prevented a true implantation of

the Christian faith in that immense country. And we turn the page over in order to understand all the better what Mao has written there—in words that have fascinated many among us. We do not know what has become of the Christians of China, and that is a shame. They still are the buried seed from which one day great harvests of faith will be gathered.

This turning in on ourselves has had its consequences. Our vision became very narrow. A returned missionary said humorously but tellingly: "The French learn in school that the earth is round but they look on it as hexagonal." Our way of looking at things reduced them to our own dimensions. This myopia can deteriorate to blindness when there is question of catching sight of God's work in the world.

World Citizens

Christians, really, cannot but be world citizens. In the very best and most important meaning of the term, that is what "catholic" signifies. As members of the church, we were born— maybe we have forgotten this—when a great wind swept over those gathered from all corners of the world, such as they knew it. The first Christians did not stand there paralyzed, their feet rooted to the ground, when the Lord ascended into heaven. No, they went everywhere telling others what had happened to them. The most forceful of them all, the Apostle of the Gentiles, managed to accomplish more in his day than we can in ours despite our Concordes and Boeings that take us all over the planet in a matter of hours.

Pope John Paul II, in his visits to the continents of the world, has placed himself in the tradition of St. Paul. This traveling pope is not a tourist; he is being carried along by the same wind that became a storm at that dawning of the church that we call Pentecost. It is wrong to think that missionary activity is out of date, and more mistaken still to decide that it should desist.

When will we take steps to cure ourselves of the amnesia that makes us confuse all of history with just one of its periods, that of Western colonization? This period itself is looked upon too simplistically. Mission was a very different thing from colonization. It is a fact that the era of the soldier and the merchant coincided with that of the missionary, but temporal coincidence is not convergence of motive. It was in the name of the gospel that men and women went to Africa, Asia, the islands of the Pacific—wherever the word had not yet been preached. The life expectancy of the missionaries who went to Africa less than a century ago was three years. There is still something extremely moving in visiting certain African cemeteries where the missionary pioneers lie at rest. They were the sowers of the faith that gave birth to those Christian communities of which the church today is so proud.

From the seed sown in all those lands many trees have grown, and they can be judged by their fruits. They are all the churches throughout the world that are bearing witness—often at great cost to themselves—to their love for Jesus Christ. Do we not have much to learn from the faith that these churches are living out? Is it not, in effect, the church's great act of faith in our days?

The apostle John tells us that if he were to record all that the Lord said and did, all the books in the world would not be sufficient. Michel Bavarel knows this better than anyone else. Throughout all his journeys he has gleaned the fruits of faith out of which he has made and presented the sheaf preserved in these pages. But the church is rich in many other sheaves, which have not been gathered into the granary of this book. We are a long way from having christianized the whole world. Only one person in three has accepted the proclamation of the kingdom. Nevertheless, everywhere, or nearly everywhere, fires have been lit. The specific goal of missionary activity today is not only to propagate the faith, as we used to say, but to marvel at seeing the faith at work in circumstances that are often difficult in the extreme.

Christians on Trial

In the pages that you have read, you often met Christians who were being put to the test. This is not an isolated phenomenon; it is a sign of our times. We are contemporaries of more martyrs than there were throughout the whole previous history of Christianity. Obviously there is nothing more missionary than a witness to the faith that goes that far. From the very beginning, the blood of martyrs has nurtured the seed of Christian growth.

In the U.S.S.R., as in so many of the countries of what we call "the East," Christians are forcibly restricted to the few churches that they are allowed to keep open. People cannot practice their faith without stirring up suspicions and compromising their future and their freedom. Nevertheless, the Christian churches are not on the way to extinction in those parts of the world where atheism is triumphant and persecutive. The greatest concentration of convinced believers is probably to be found in Russia, which Cardinal Etchegaray, a few years ago, called a "spiritual volcano." In many other places as well, Christians find themselves restricted. It is for the same justice, the same gospel, the same faith that Christians are suffering in Eastern Europe, in China, Korea, El Salvador, Guatemala, Guinea—in every place where human and divine rights are made light of. Regimes that practice oppression or the exploitation of human beings pursue their goals for reasons that may be completely divergent. But the result is always the same: they do violence to believers as well as to all those who struggle to maintain their human dignity.

In more than one part of the world it is hard to be a Christian, and often it is forbidden to practice the faith openly. Still, the church is never more missionary than in those places where the gospel is forbidden. Making the good news known is not dependent upon what we do but upon that which the Spirit gives us to live out. Moreover, there is a mysterious law by which the church purifies itself in the crucible of trial. Human liberation in the East will not come about by the rejection of God but by the rediscovery of him. In Russia, God has once again become a problem vastly more serious than all the hackneyed doctrines about him, notwithstanding all their pretensions.

The purification of the church in Latin America, in Asia, and in Africa is being carried out through the rediscovery of the poor, in the gospel sense of that term. The justice due them is a strict right and not something to be accorded condescendingly. This is important when we consider the exemplary struggle on the part of priests, bishops, religious, and Christian lay persons in Latin America. Despite what Marx was able to say about it, the word of God is not opium there, but a powerful trumpet call. The word makes persons stand up, it makes them aware of the dignity that they have from God, in whose image they were created.

In Latin America, as everywhere else, we are rediscovering the power of the Magnificat that exalts the humble and brings down the mighty from their thrones. It was not wrong or in vain for John Paul II to have made the Magnificat the backbone of an address he gave to the workers of St. Denis and many other places as well. The Spirit of God, the tireless missionary, is at work, awakening his church and those who have charge of it. It was not by chance that Oscar Romero, a genuine martyr of our times, was prepared for his destiny. God led him where he never thought of going. Jesus said to Peter, "Another will gird you and lead you," and that continues to be the pattern in our day.

Africa has no fewer problems and it is also a land of martyrs. The church from its very beginnings in Uganda underwent a baptism of blood, and it united Catholics and Anglicans in the same sacrifice. This helped to show us that God is always ahead of us on whatever road we take, including where, in our disunity, we still hesitate. Many Christians are suffering in Africa in many different ways, and troubles are evolving there that will affect our whole planet.

There are as well Christians who have no choice. They will have to be against racism in those places where it is law. They will have to oppose those totalitarian regimes that want to rule over everything. The African church has enriched the universal church with confessors of the faith who have not retreated when faced with death or prison. Raymond Marie Tchidimbo spent eight years and eight months in prison without weakening; on the contrary, he grew in that faith from which he now enriches us all. The tiny church in Guinea, as well as that of China, is another example to us. Christians are but a tiny modicum of the population in those places but their influence is out of all proportion to their size. Christians have to be reckoned by their faith, not by their numbers.

The Great Challenge

According to the evidence, Africa is a land rich in promise for Christianity. It is on that continent that Christianity has known the most rapid expansion in all its history. There are one hundred million Christians there today, and there will be two or three times that number in the next century if the curve continues to follow its predictable trajectory. Obviously, Christianity is no longer something riveted to the West. In Africa, as in Asia, Christianity stands on a common meeting ground with the other great religions of the world. This will be the great challenge of tomorrow. We cannot take up this challenge with a crusader mentality, despite all the temptations history offers us to go backward. This is the moment of encounter, the moment of truth and of faith, for all the believers of the world. Christians who live in a region of Africa dominated by Islam are not there to convert it. Rather, they are there to live even more deeply the mystery of that God whose transcendence their Moslem brothers and sisters recall to them, and whose gentle presence they know so well. It is to be found in the name and in the countenance of Jesus Christ. Coexistence with Islam calls Christians to a greater faith. They need to live their experience of prayer and of faith with that of all their co-believers throughout the world. Communion among all the disciples of Jesus is a matter of strict necessity and in our days it takes the form of mutual sharing.

The gospel that we once carried elsewhere is now being brought back to us. The more one gives, the richer one becomes in the kingdom where we are all given the fullness of God. At the dawn of this century, when faith was no longer axiomatic, at least not for us Westerners, great Christian heroes lived in Africa. There was de Foucauld, and Peyriguiere, to name but two. They became the brothers of all men and women, and we have not finished plumbing the depths of their message and drawing nourishment from it. It is in Africa as well, in daily interaction, that Islam and Christianity, which are not meant to be blended together, must live all that is demanded of them to its very fullest. It is at that point that he who is "the way, the truth, and the life" awaits them. Nothing that is truly lived can be lost; in this, Africa contains great spiritual wealth.

Asia is no less a meeting ground between other religions and the disciples of Jesus, though they are less numerous there. For some time now, India has become something of a missionary for young Westerners looking for themselves and their souls. They had access to the only water that could fully quench their thirst, but they did not know how to draw it. Or perhaps we kept it too jealously guarded in a reservoir where it had begun to stagnate. India needs Christians who know how to discover its riches without plundering them. The way has been opened by Fr. Montchanin and others like him. Mother Teresa, Indian by adoption and in her heart, is, in Calcutta and a hundred other places, a presence that speaks to everyone. India, like the rest of the world, needs Christians for whom love is not a word but a name.

China deserves more of our attention. Marxism, that child of the West, has made it go through a mill that—so it claims—has recast it. In any case the belief that human nature can do everything by itself is Western enough.

We are now beginning to appreciate the cost of that experiment and it is no less than what one finds elsewhere. Mao now reposes in his mausoleum and everyone is trying to forget him, if not denounce him. The regime will no doubt continue in the same basic direction for quite a while. It is certainly not characterized by any spiritual preoccupations, but this does not mean that such preoccupations are not returning in force to the people. Thirty years of a hope that never was realized digs out a void and steals the soul of a people. There is hunger for God and a hunger for one's own soul in a country where some thought it would suffice to assure everyone a bowl of rice. The Christians who remained in the shadows—the true people of God— guaranteed that the faith was never totally absent. All their priests are elderly and have passed through prison. Their freedom is still under strict control. Nevertheless, these Christians who were cut off from everything kept the faith and in their catacombs wrote a new chapter in the history of the church. They are not at the end of the tunnel yet, but God will not forsake them. When relations are finally reestablished with the universal church, we will not be going there to bring them something. We have everything to receive from them—and on our knees, always the correct posture when there is question of thanking God for his work in our fellow Christians.

The Gospel Comes from Elsewhere

We can learn from all this that the gospel always comes to us from somewhere else. This serves to remind us that we are not really from this place or that; rather, we belong to the one kingdom that can lay its claim on every human being. The West was more deeply marked by Christianity than it thinks, but it has declared its independence. Christians in this part of the world feel, sometimes to the point of anguish, the solitude of the faith. But perhaps they have not been sufficiently sensitive to the malaise that seized upon preceeding generations, including the most ancient.

We have dominated the world but we are not equal to it. What kind of a power is it that can delay death but not overcome it?

Our self-sufficiency and our arrogance fell far short of our true destiny and its mystery. Unbelief is still the dominant law among us but it cannot hide its insufficiency. There is a fissure somewhere in that Western humanity that proclaimed itself all-powerful and now finds itself in despair. In the end, Christians have not succumbed to all the shocks of seeing the faith being put on trial, of hearing questions directed to its very foundation, of having doubt erected as an absolute. Despite everything, faith has remained. Now, it is deeper and purer. It is willing, like Abraham, the father of all believers, to set out relying only on the word of God.

Christians in the West as elsewhere have things to say to others—things that are essential for their life. We are not overnight guests. The earth is inhabited by the God of mercy who wishes to make his dwelling place within us. At a time when humanity is doubting its very soul, this is not an irrelevant scrap of information.

•

Mission is a movement that comes from faith. What we hear whispered in our ear we must go and proclaim in the marketplace. The gospel is an experience that propels us out to the limits of the world and the limits of our own resources. The task is never accomplished once for all; it must continually be begun again. We cannot stop because of failure: the whole history of the church is full of failures. But the faith and the holiness that truly make the church do not come from human nature.

Missionaries, it is true, could only see so far. But they kept on going, in faith. Even when they had to grope their way, they planted the church, and believers rose up in the breath of the Spirit. God made them capable of anything, and we marvel at it. We have to keep our gaze outward, at the immense throng of humanity where God awaits us and where he has preceded us.

Faith is the world in its youth, and it alone bears its future. Christians cannot keep this faith for themselves, but neither can they talk in words alone. By their whole life and their whole faith they must become both word and mission.

9505